THE ART & SCIENCE OF CSS

BY **CAMERON ADAMS**
JINA BOLTON
DAVID JOHNSON
STEVE SMITH
JONATHAN SNOOK

Expert Reviewer: Dan Rubin

Expert Reviewer: Jared Christensen

Technical Editor: Andrew Krespanis

Editor: Hilary Reynolds

Cover Design: Alex Walker

Production: *Book*NZ (www.booknz.co.nz)

Managing Editor: Simon Mackie

Technical Director: Kevin Yank

Index Editor: Max McMaster

Printing History

First Edition: March 2007

Published by SitePoint Pty. Ltd.

424 Smith Street Collingwood

VIC Australia 3066.

Web: www.sitepoint.com

Email: business@sitepoint.com

ISBN 978-0-9758419-7-6

Printed and bound in Canada

About the Authors

Cameron Adams has been adding to the Internet for over seven years and now runs his own design and development business. He likes to combine the aesthetic with the technological on his weblog, http://www.themaninblue.com/, which contains equal parts of JavaScript, design, and CSS.

Jina Bolton, interactive designer, holds a Bachelor of Fine Arts degree in Computer Arts and Graphic Design from Memphis College of Art. In addition to being featured in *CSS Professional Style* and *Web Designing* magazine, Jina consults for various agencies and organizations, including the World Wide Web Consortium. She enjoys traveling, is learning Italian, and considers herself a sushi enthusiast.

David Johnson is one of those evil .NET developers from Melbourne, Australia. He is the senior developer at Lemonade, http://www.lemonade.com.au/, and his role includes C# programming, database design using SQL Server, and front-end development using XHTML and CSS. He makes up for his evil deeds by being a firm believer in web standards and accessibility, and forcing .NET to abide by these rules. His favourite candy is Sherbies.

Steve Smith lives with his wife, son, and a few miscellaneous animals in South Bend, Indiana, USA. As well as maintaining his personal web site, http://orderedlist.com/, Steve works as an independent web designer, developer, and consultant. He does his best to convince his clients and friends that web standards should be a way of life.

Jonathan Snook has been involved with the Web since '95, and is lucky to be able to call his hobby a career. He worked in web agencies for over six years and has worked with high-profile clients in government, the private sector, and non-profit organizations. Jonathan Snook currently runs his own web development business from Ottawa, Canada, and continues to write about what he loves on his blog, http://snook.ca/.

About the Expert Reviewers

Dan Rubin is a published author, consultant, and speaker on user interface design, usability, and web standards development. His portfolio and writings can be found on http://superfluousbanter.org/ and http://webgraph.com/.

Jared Christensen is a user experience designer and the proprietor of http://jaredigital.com. He has been drawing and designing since the day he could hold a crayon; he enjoys elegant code, walks in the park, and a well-made sandwich.

About the Technical Editor

Andrew Krespanis moved to web development after tiring of the instant noodles that form the diet of the struggling musician. When he's not diving headfirst into new web technologies, he's tending his bonsai, playing jazz guitar, and occasionally posting to his personal site, http://leftjustified.net/.

About the Technical Director

As Technical Director for SitePoint, Kevin Yank oversees all of its technical publications—books, articles, newsletters, and blogs. He has written over 50 articles for SitePoint, but is best known for his book, *Build Your Own Database Driven Website Using PHP & MySQL*. Kevin lives in Melbourne, Australia, and enjoys performing improvised comedy theater and flying light aircraft.

About SitePoint

SitePoint specializes in publishing fun, practical, and easy-to-understand content for web professionals. Visit http://www.sitepoint.com/ to access our books, newsletters, articles, and community forums.

Table of Contents

Preface

In the early days of CSS, many web designers associated it with boring, square boxes and thin borders. "CSS is *ugly*!" they would cry. It took projects such as CSS Edge[1] and CSS Zen Garden[2] to show the web design world that not only could CSS designs achieve the same aesthetic qualities of their table-based ancestors, but, furthermore, that new and interesting design possibilities were available. Not to mention how much more maintainable the markup is—imagine how very, very happy you'll be if you never again have to stare down the barrel of another day's worth of **table** hacking!

Each chapter of this book will teach you how to style common web site components through practical examples. Along the way, you'll learn many handy techniques for bringing complex designs to life in all modern browsers without needing to resort to messy hacks or superfluous presentational markup. Neither accessibility nor markup quality should be sacrificed to make tricky designs easier to achieve, so the exercises you'll find in this book all use examples of best practice XHTML and CSS. Each chapter progressively builds upon the skills you'll have acquired in previous exercises, giving you a practical toolkit of skills with which to express your own creative ideas.

Who Should Read this Book?

This book is ideal for anyone who wants to gain the practical skills involved in using CSS to make attractive web sites, especially if you're not the type who likes to learn by memorizing a formal specification and then trying to work out which browsers implemented it completely (does *anyone* enjoy reading specifications?). The only knowledge you'll need to have is some familiarity with HTML. This book will give designers the skills they need to implement their ideas, and provides developers with creative inspiration through practical examples.

What's in this Book?

This book contains seven chapters that engage with the fundamental elements of the web page—headings, images, backgrounds, navigation—as well as applied styles such as those used in forms, rounded corners for content boxes, and tables. CSS is inherent in the approaches we'll use in the exercises presented here. These exercises will encourage you to address the questions of art and science in all the design choices you make, as a means to

---

1   http://meyerweb.com/eric/css/edge/
2   http://csszengarden.com/

create designs that are as beautiful as they are functional. Throughout the book, therefore, considerations of usability are always paramount—both in terms of users of mainstream browsers and those employing assistive technology.

Chapter 1: Headings

Simultaneously conveying the content and the identity of your site, headings are truly the attention-grabbers of your web page. With only a handful of fonts being available across all browsers, CSS can help you style headings that stand out from the crowd. In this chapter, Cameron Adams will show you how to use image and Flash replacement to gain unlimited creativity in designing headings, while retaining the page's accessibility across all browsers.

Chapter 2: Images

Images are the windows to your web page's soul. Jina Bolton will teach you stunning ways to display your images as she walks you through a number of attractive examples. You'll learn to create a photo album, as well as to successfully place introductory and in-content images within your pages. The techniques of applying borders, padding, typography, and colors to best present your work are covered in detail in this chapter. You'll also discover effective ways to style those all-important captions.

Chapter 3: Backgrounds

You've probably already found that CSS has significantly affected the way you use web page backgrounds. Here, David Johnson will explain the properties you'll use on a daily basis to transfer your design visions into light-weight markup and CSS. You'll then work through a case study for a fictional project, in which you'll create a great-looking design that's well supported by all modern browsers. Finally, we'll look to the future to predict the new background capabilities that CSS 3 will bring!

Chapter 4: Navigation

Navigation is crucial to your users' experience of your web site. Steve Smith will reveal the secrets of successful navigation through a case study involving a fictional design client. You'll build both basic and advanced applications of the main navigation styles in use today, including horizontal, vertical, and tabbed navigation menus, and discover how you can use CSS styling to make your navigation both beautiful and usable.

Chapter 5: Forms

Forms are the quiet achievers of the web page. In this chapter, Cameron Adams will help you ensure that your forms are available to all users—even those employing assistive technology. You'll learn how to create an attractive form that will allow for the correct and effective labeling, grouping, layout, and styling of your form elements. Forms needn't be just a tedious necessity—as you'll learn in this chapter, they can be presented in a way that enhances your site's overall impact.

Chapter 6: Rounded Corners

Those sharp corners on HTML content boxes have been the bane of many a web designer's life for years. But CSS has changed all that, as Steve Smith explains. Flexibility is the key—horizontal, vertical, or even a combination of both forms— to creating rounded corners for your boxes with some straightforward styling. The achievement of rounded corners does hold traps for the unwary, including unsympathetic browsers, but you'll find that taking the few small precautions detailed here will help you to avoid them.

Chapter 7: Tables

Tables have gained a new lease of life in the CSS era—while they've finally been freed from misuse as a layout element, they retain enormous potential as presenters of data. Jonathan Snook will demonstrate how you can use CSS to create exciting, colorful tables, which will work successfully across browsers. You'll also be invited to envision the future, in which the advent of the wide use of CSS 3 will create even more scope for creative tables.

This Book's Web Site

Located at http://www.sitepoint.com/books/cssdesign1/, the web site supporting this book will give you access to the following facilities.

The Code Archive

The code archive for this book, which can be downloaded from http://www.sitepoint.com/books/cssdesign1/code.php, contains the source code and images for each and every example in this book.

Updates and Errata

The Corrections and Typos page on the book's web site, at http://www.sitepoint.com/books/cssdesign1/errata.php, will always have the latest information about known typographical and code errors, and necessary updates for changes to technologies.

The SitePoint Forums

While we've made every attempt to anticipate any questions you may have, and answer them in this book, there is no way that any publication could cover everything there is to know about designing with CSS. If you have a question about anything in this book, the best place to go for a quick answer is SitePoint's Forums, at http://www.sitepoint.com/forums/—SitePoint's vibrant and knowledgeable community.

The SitePoint Newsletters

In addition to books like this one, SitePoint offers free email newsletters. The *SitePoint Tech Times* covers the latest news, product releases, trends, tips, and techniques for all technical aspects of web development. The long-running *SitePoint Tribune* is a biweekly digest of the business and moneymaking aspects of the Web. Whether you're a freelance developer looking for tips to score that dream contract, or a marketing major striving to keep abreast of changes to the major search engines, this is the newsletter for you. The *SitePoint Design View* is a monthly compilation of the best in web design. From new CSS layout methods to subtle Photoshop techniques, SitePoint's chief designer shares his years of experience in its pages. Browse the archives or sign up to any of SitePoint's free newsletters at http://www.sitepoint.com/newsletter/.

Your Feedback

If you can't find your answer through the forums, or you wish to contact us for any other reason, the best place to write is books@sitepoint.com. SitePoint has a well-manned email support system set up to track your inquiries, and if the support staff are unable to answer your question, they send it straight to us. Suggestions for improvement as well as notices of any mistakes you may find are especially welcome.

Headings

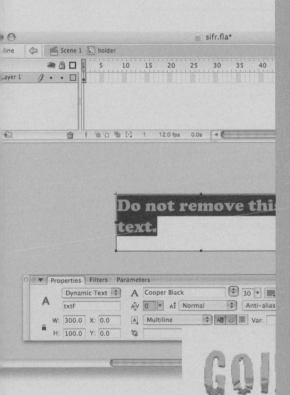

As your eyes skim over the streams of Arial on the Internet, it's the headings that catch your attention, like shiny nickels lying in the dust.

You may think that headings are tiny in the scheme of things, but their impact amidst all that body text is profound. Naturally, they draw attention—that's their purpose. Either they give the reader a quick idea of what the slabs of text underneath them contain, or they describe the structure of an article, or they impart some more abstract sense of the content—through shape, size, or color, as well as their actual content.

However, there's a lot more to headings than meets the eye, and so we'll consider them from all angles in this chapter.

We'll look at what you need to think about when designing them for your site, and what function they need to perform. We'll learn from some examples that demonstrate how headings convey the identity of the site in question. And we'll see that you can go crazy with your design, by all means. Before you let your creativity all hang out, though, there are a few cautionary measures you'll need to take to make sure your site's users see your efforts the way you intend. For the most part, this chapter is concerned with the careful coding of headings in order to avoid all sorts of potential problems.

Hierarchy

One function of headings is to define the hierarchy of a web page. The semantics behind HTML document structure naturally include some sense of hierarchy, with headings ranging from the big and bold **h1** to the diminutive **h6**. However, from a visual perspective, it's the task of the designer to indicate this hierarchy so that the site retains a sense of design and personality.

Khoi Vinh's web site, Subtraction, which you can see in Figure 1.1, is an excellent example of using just font size and weight on headings to create an immediate sense of hierarchy on the page.[1]

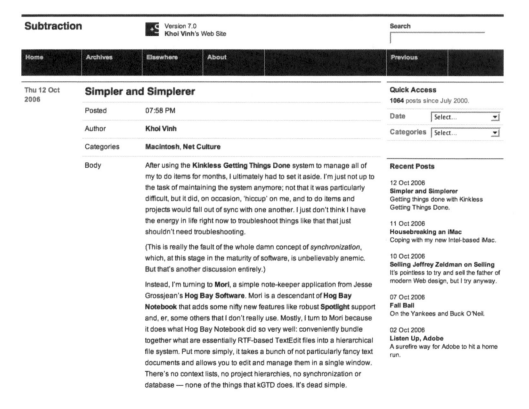

Figure 1.1: Use of font sizing and weight on heading text

The layout grid for this site also helps to create a visual structure, but what if we were to convert the structure of the page into a linear layout? As shown in Figure 1.2, the headings themselves still convey a lot of the information required by the user while retaining the site's character—insofar as Helvetica can adequately express a site's character all by itself nowadays!

---

1   http://www.subtraction.com/

Figure 1.2: Layout grid removed

As you'll see in Figure 1.3, the A List Apart web site takes a very different tack from Subtraction when differentiating its headlines from its content.[2] Weight and font size are used again, but these effects are combined with different typefaces, colors, and capitalization for the article headings and author names.

Figure 1.3: Use of typefaces, font size and colors to differentiate headings

At first glance, it could be said that the A List Apart headlines are more differentiated than those on the Subtraction site, but at the end of the day it's all about what style ties into a site's particular design. Subtraction's style is more conservative and minimalist, A List Apart's more ornate. The designers of both sites have done excellent work in creating a visual hierarchy within the respective frameworks.

Because of the well-formed semantics underlying this visual hierarchy, CSS is well suited to manipulating the appearance of each and every heading to produce the visual effects we require for a clear structure.

However, hierarchy is but one aspect of headings. Let's look at that other, more elusive, aspect—identity.

Identity

The key to creating a memorable site is to stamp it with a distinct identity, one that visitors will remember and associate with your content or services. And in order for your identity to be memorable, it has to be unique.

With a medium such as the Web, visual design is a strong expression of identity. It'll come as no surprise that your company logo has to be unique. Likewise, your site design—colors, layout, images—must be unique. Your headings are an integral part of that formation of identity, as a reflection of your site design; they should have some nuance that makes your site special and different.

To consider headings is to consider typography. The current state of HTML typography on the Web is improving, but it's still poor. Only an extremely limited number of fonts have the widespread distribution necessary to be reliably represented in any browser. If you examine most surveys of fonts available on users' computers, all you'll find is a weary list of familiar faces (sorry, pun intended): Arial, Times New Roman, Courier, Trebuchet, Lucida, Georgia, Garamond … and we're already down to the fonts that only 75% of users have![3]

With such a limited range of fonts, how can you differentiate your site from the next one? If they're all using Arial, you can use Trebuchet, but that's about as far out as you can go. If you use Trebuchet, what can the next designer who seeks to be different use? Multiply this situation by a billion sites or so, and we're looking at quite a homogeneous Web.

Body text can get away with being just a face in the crowd. If your users are to be reading

---

3   http://www.visibone.com/font/FontResults.html

any amount of text, you don't want any fancy bells and whistles for it; it just needs to be readable and easy on the eyes. So we merely have to make a fairly undemanding choice between serif and sans serif for body text. But when it comes to headings, we'd like some style. We *need* some style.

However, you don't have to be outlandish and in-your-face when designing your headings in order to stand out from the crowd. Often the key is subtlety; a well-harmonized typeface can bring about the greatest effect, as is evident on the Rapha site shown in Figure 1.4.[4]

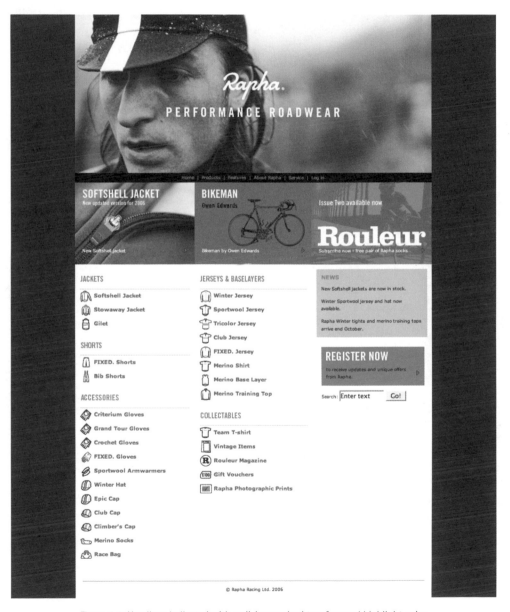

Figure 1.4: Headings indicated with well-harmonized typeface and highlight color

4   http://www.rapha.cc/

The combination of Rapha's script-style logotype with its clean, modern headings evokes the spirit of classic bicycle racing with a contemporary edge, which is very effective in creating an identity unique to its products.

But, if you do want to go crazy, there's countless typefaces, treatments, and effects you can apply to your headings to make them fit in with your design concept and give your site that unique touch, as the Altoids homepage has done so effectively in Figure 1.5.

Figure 1.5: Outlandish headings can work too!

This site has headings with a number of typefaces, each with different effects—bending, fills, ornamentation, outlines, drop shadows—that powerfully reinforce the vaudeville theme of Altoids.

So, if we've only got a limited number of fonts to use in a browser, but we want to use an infinite variety of fonts on our web pages, what are the solutions?

Image Replacement

There are almost as many techniques for image replacement as there are web developers. The concept behind all these image replacement tricks is that the text normally displayed by HTML is hidden and replaced by an image. This means that any user with a CSS-enabled browser will see the replaced text, but user agents that don't support CSS will just see the plain text.

Let's say we have some HTML like this:

```
<h1>
  Going to the snow!
</h1>
<p>
…
</p>
```

Our aim is to hide the text of the level 1 heading—"Going to the snow!"—and replace it with an image.

There are many different ways of using image replacement. All have their advantages and disadvantages, but here are the two most useful ones.

Using Text-indent

With `text-indent` image replacement, a negative `text-indent` is used on the text inside the heading element to make it move off the left edge of the screen, effectively placing it out of view.

CSS is then used to put a background image inside the **h1**, which means that your heading can adopt any design you like.

Why is a negative `text-indent` necessary? We could just declare the properties that display the background image:

```
h1 {
  height: 43px;
  background-image: url(images/title_snow.gif);
  background-repeat: no-repeat;
}
```

But the HTML text of the heading would still be visible, as shown in Figure 1.6.

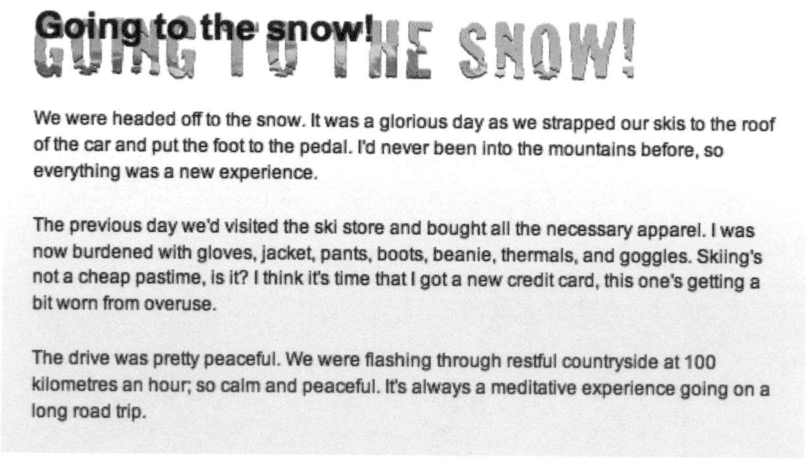

Figure 1.6: Without negative text-indentation—HTML text appears on top of background image

So that's why we provide some negative text-indentation—to move the text waaaaay to the left:

```
                                                    text-indent.css (excerpt)
h1 {
  height: 43px;
  background-image: url(images/title_snow.gif);
  background-repeat: no-repeat;
  text-indent: -9999px;
}
```

The value that we use to indent the text is kind of arbitrary. All we need to do is move it far enough to the left so that it won't appear on the screen. As -9999 pixels will cover almost any page width and text length, it's a good value to use by default, as well as being easy to type.

In addition to the `text-indent`, a `height` that corresponds to the height of the image has to be set on the `h1`. This ensures that the `h1` is tall enough to show the entire image, in a situation where the natural height of the element would clip it.

Once the text is indented, the title displays nicely—a feat that would otherwise be impossible to achieve with HTML. Figure 1.7 shows how the heading looks in the browser.

NOTE *Overflow*

You may also want to set **overflow: hidden** on the **h1**, for the case where the natural height of the **h1** may be too big for the image. Although most standards-based browsers will adhere to the specified **height** in this situation, Internet Explorer 6 and below will expand to fit the content, so your **h1** may end up larger than the image, producing too much whitespace. Setting **overflow: hidden** will prevent this problem.

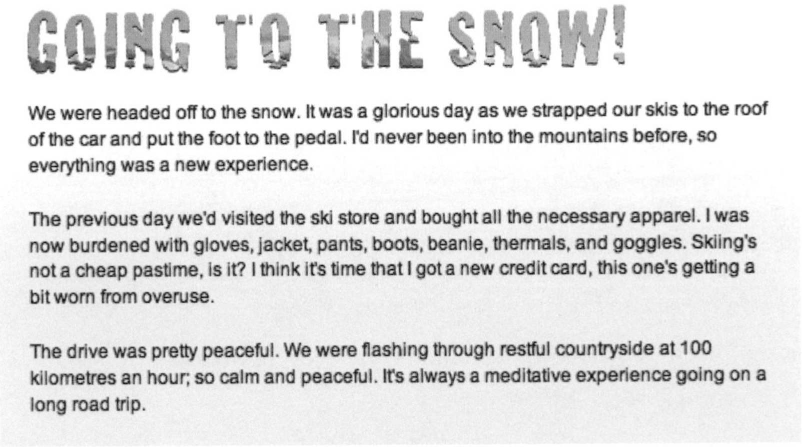

GOING TO THE SNOW!

We were headed off to the snow. It was a glorious day as we strapped our skis to the roof of the car and put the foot to the pedal. I'd never been into the mountains before, so everything was a new experience.

The previous day we'd visited the ski store and bought all the necessary apparel. I was now burdened with gloves, jacket, pants, boots, beanie, thermals, and goggles. Skiing's not a cheap pastime, is it? I think it's time that I got a new credit card, this one's getting a bit worn from overuse.

The drive was pretty peaceful. We were flashing through restful countryside at 100 kilometres an hour; so calm and peaceful. It's always a meditative experience going on a long road trip.

Figure 1.7: HTML page with image-replaced heading

There is, however, one disadvantage of `text-indent` image replacement. If the image doesn't display, there'll be a meaningless gap in the page, as shown in Figure 1.8. This means that users who may have CSS turned on but images turned off—or even users who are just waiting for the image to download—won't see any alternative text, so they'll have no idea what the heading is.

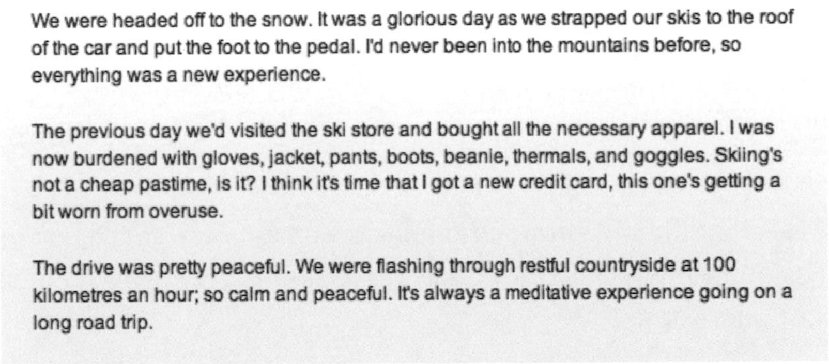

We were headed off to the snow. It was a glorious day as we strapped our skis to the roof of the car and put the foot to the pedal. I'd never been into the mountains before, so everything was a new experience.

The previous day we'd visited the ski store and bought all the necessary apparel. I was now burdened with gloves, jacket, pants, boots, beanie, thermals, and goggles. Skiing's not a cheap pastime, is it? I think it's time that I got a new credit card, this one's getting a bit worn from overuse.

The drive was pretty peaceful. We were flashing through restful countryside at 100 kilometres an hour; so calm and peaceful. It's always a meditative experience going on a long road trip.

Figure 1.8: Image replacement with images turned off—no alternative text showing

Our second solution caters specifically for this scenario.

Providing Additional Markup

The way to provide "alternative" text for those users without images enabled is to leave the HTML text where it is, but physically hide it using an image. So, instead of moving the text itself, we cover it up with the image we're using to replace it. The image will appear to those users who have images enabled, while the text will display for those who don't.

This technique requires us to use a small amount of additional markup inside the **h1**:

additional-markup.html (excerpt)

```
<h1>
  <span></span>Going to the snow!
</h1>
```

The extra **span** inside the **h1** gives us an element to which we can apply a background image to cover up the HTML text.

We do this by positioning the **span** absolutely:

additional-markup.css (excerpt)

```
h1 {
  position: relative;
  width: 389px;
  height: 43px;
  overflow: hidden;
}
h1 span {
  position: absolute;
  left: 0;
  top: 0;
  width: 100%;
  height: 100%;
  background-image: url(images/title_snow.gif);
  background-repeat: no-repeat;
}
```

Positioning the **span** absolutely moves it from the document flow, so the text of the **h1** will naturally flow underneath it. Once the **background-image** has been moved onto this **span**, the **span** will cover up the **h1**'s text.

The **h1** is positioned relatively because any absolutely positioned elements nested inside a relatively positioned element will base their origin coordinates on the relatively positioned parent. Consequently, when the **span**'s **left** position is set to **0** and **top** position to **0** it will position itself at the top left of the **h1**, instead of relative to the entire page.

In addition to changing the **h1**'s position, we explicitly set its **height** and **width**, and set **overflow** to **hidden**. The HTML text remains in its normal position, so if the text grows beyond the dimensions of the image, it will begin to peek out from behind the image. To prevent this problem we make the **h1** exactly the same size as the image, and use **overflow: hidden** to cut off any text that exceeds the boundaries of the **h1**.

Also, the **span** must be the same size as the image if all of the image is to be displayed; we set the **height** and **width** of the **span** to 100% so that it will automatically expand to the size of the **h1**. We could explicitly set its size in pixels, but, using the technique I've shown here, we only have to enter the exact pixel size on the **h1**—it's always nice to save time on maintenance!

This method produces exactly the same result as the **text-indent** image replacement technique. The only difference, which you can see in Figure 1.9, is that if the image is turned off, users will still see relevant text there to tell them what the title's meant to be.

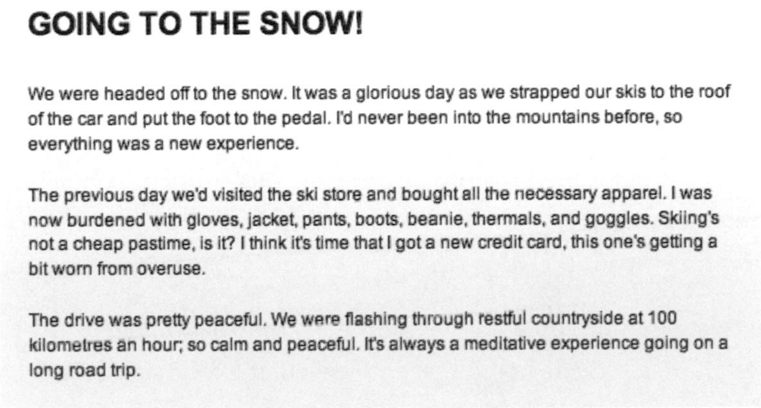

GOING TO THE SNOW!

We were headed off to the snow. It was a glorious day as we strapped our skis to the roof of the car and put the foot to the pedal. I'd never been into the mountains before, so everything was a new experience.

The previous day we'd visited the ski store and bought all the necessary apparel. I was now burdened with gloves, jacket, pants, boots, beanie, thermals, and goggles. Skiing's not a cheap pastime, is it? I think it's time that I got a new credit card, this one's getting a bit worn from overuse.

The drive was pretty peaceful. We were flashing through restful countryside at 100 kilometres an hour; so calm and peaceful. It's always a meditative experience going on a long road trip.

Figure 1.9: Image replacement with additional markup to provide alternative text when image is not available

This text can be styled normally, as it would if we were using plain HTML headings:

additional-markup.css (excerpt)

```
h1 {
  position: relative;
  width: 389px;
  height: 43px;
  overflow: hidden;
  font-size: 175%;
  line-height: 43px;
  text-transform: uppercase;
}
```

The major disadvantage of this method is obvious—the additional markup. We're sacrificing semantic purity for accessibility and usability. It's a sacrifice I normally make willingly, to create a better experience for most users, but it's good to know that there is a "pure" markup solution if you need it. You'll have to weigh up the options as they apply to your own situation.

Flash Replacement

One major downside of image replacement is that it requires a lot of manual labor. Every heading that you want to include on a site has to be created in Photoshop, cut up, saved as an image, and included in your CSS.

If you're creating content regularly, this work can become very time consuming; sometimes it's just impossible. Imagine a site that has a content management system with multiple authors, none of whom have access to—let alone know how to *use*—a graphics program. It's simply not feasible to have someone there just to create image-replaced headings.

But what if you had a system that automatically created nice headings, in a typeface of your choice, without you having to do anything to the HTML? That would be heaven. And there *is* such a system: **sIFR**.

Scalable Inman Flash Replacement is now in its second version (with a third already in beta) and, after being around for a couple of years, is rock solid. You'll need to download some source files from the sIFR homepage in order to get it going.[5] Don't worry, I'll wait around while you download it.

sIFR works like this: you include a JavaScript file on your pages that scans for headings, copies the text from inside those headings, and uses that text inside a Flash object that replaces the HTML text. The Flash object contains the font you want, so the text is automatically formatted the way you want it, *and* you don't have to do any customization work. sIFR also scales the Flash object appropriately to fill the same amount of space that the HTML text occupied, so your text replacement will be the same size.

Technically, the HTML text isn't replaced, it's just hidden, so the text remains fully accessible. If Flash isn't available, the sIFR JavaScript detects that and leaves the page untouched; if JavaScript isn't turned on, the page will remain in its normal state. This way users see nice headings if their browsers allow it, but if their browsers don't handle these headings, they degrade to perfectly readable text.

For a beautiful example of sIFR, take a look at the Noodlebox site.[6] Noodlebox's introduction text and other headings all use a custom typeface that reinforces its identity and also produces a more refined design, as can be seen in Figure 1.10.

---

5   http://www.mikeindustries.com/sifr/
6   http://www.noodlebox.be/

Figure 1.10: Use of sIFR for introduction text and major headings

Figure 1.11 shows the result when sIFR is unavailable, due to the user's lack of either Flash or JavaScript. The HTML text acts as a backup and provides an approximation of the designer's real vision.

It's a win–win situation! Those users who have Flash and JavaScript reap the benefits; those without are none the wiser.

Figure 1.11: Backup HTML text without sIFR

Supplying Basic Markup and CSS

It's more likely with Flash replacement than with image replacement that some of your users will experience the degraded version, so you should pay careful attention to the styles that they will see if Flash and JavaScript are turned off.

Let's imagine that the font we'd *really* like to use for our **h1** headings is Cooper Black, but we know that not many people have that on their computers. Instead, we'll have those users view our headings in Georgia, or some similar serif font:

flash-replacement.css (excerpt)

```
h1 {
  color: #06C;
  font-size: 250%;
  font-family: Georgia, serif;
  line-height: 1.45em;
}
```

The basic page looks like Figure 1.12.

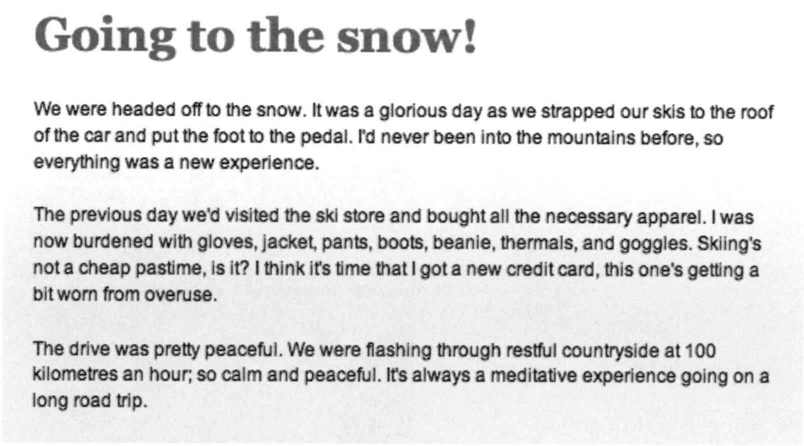

Going to the snow!

We were headed off to the snow. It was a glorious day as we strapped our skis to the roof of the car and put the foot to the pedal. I'd never been into the mountains before, so everything was a new experience.

The previous day we'd visited the ski store and bought all the necessary apparel. I was now burdened with gloves, jacket, pants, boots, beanie, thermals, and goggles. Skiing's not a cheap pastime, is it? I think it's time that I got a new credit card, this one's getting a bit worn from overuse.

The drive was pretty peaceful. We were flashing through restful countryside at 100 kilometres an hour; so calm and peaceful. It's always a meditative experience going on a long road trip.

Figure 1.12: Basically styled page that users without Flash or JavaScript will see

Time to make it all Coopery!

Supplying the Typeface

The quest to allow web users access to a wider range of fonts on HTML pages has been regularly thwarted by patchy browser implementations and the legalities of sharing typefaces. sIFR circumvents these limitations by embedding a particular typeface inside a Flash file. In order to use a particular font on your site, you have to open up the special sIFR Flash template and create a new *.swf* file that copies the font from your computer.

> **NOTE   *sIFR and Whitespace***
>
> sIFR can be affected by extra whitespace inside your HTML tags. For code readability, I normally write my HTML like this:
>
> ```
> <h1>
>   Going to the snow!
> </h1>
> ```
>
> The actual HTML text is on a new line and indented one more tabstop than the tag itself. However, with sIFR, that whitespace that appears before the HTML text will produce a one-character space at the beginning of the Flash replacement—not good! To use this technique, you'll need to code your HTML as follows:
>
> ```
> <h1>Going to the snow!</h1>
> ```
>
> No spaces, no worries.

It's really easy to do this. As shown in Figure 1.13, we just open up `sifr.fla`, select the text object on the stage (the one that says "Do not remove this text"), and change its font to the one we need. Then, when we publish that movie as a *.swf*, it will contain all the data needed to reproduce the headings in that font.

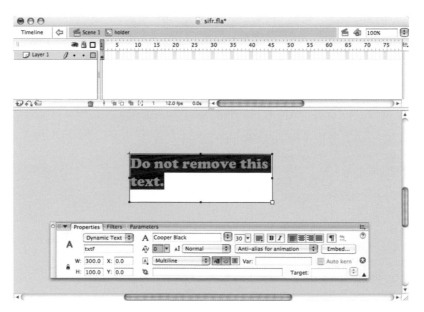

Figure 1.13: The one-step process of preparing the sIFR *.swf* file

> **NOTE   *"But I Don't Have the Flash IDE!"***
>
> Don't have the IDE? Never fear, multiple repositories of precompiled sIFR *.swf*s are available on the Internet, giving those users without the Flash IDE a wide range of fonts to choose from. In fact, one of them happens to be maintained by an author of this book![7]

---

7   http://www.fontsmack.com/

You should generally call your .*swf* files by the fonts that they include, so that you can identify them easily later. As we've just created a .*swf* for the Cooper Black font, we could call the .*swf* file `cooper_black.swf`.

Once we have this .*swf*, it's ready to be included on the web page.

Customizing the JavaScript

There's one script file that we need to include on the web page, and that's `sifr.js`—you'll find it in the package you downloaded from the official sIFR site. To start out, it just needs to be inserted in the head of your page:

flash-replacement.html (excerpt)

```
<script type="text/javascript" src="scripts/sifr.js"></script>
```

You'll need to take a look inside the JavaScript file to configure the file specifically for the site. You don't need to be concerned with most of it—it's 11KB of tricky Flash detection and DOM manipulation—but right at the bottom you'll see these few lines:

```
If (typeof sIFR == "function" && !sIFR.UA.bIsIEMac)
{
  sIFR.setup();
}
```

Don't remove any of that code; you'll have to insert some of your own code in order to indicate which headings you want to replace and what you want to replace them with:

scripts/sifr.js (excerpt)

```
if(typeof sIFR == "function" && !sIFR.UA.bIsIEMac)
{
  sIFR.setup();
  sIFR.replaceElement(named({sSelector: "h1",
    sFlashSrc: "flash/cooper_black.swf", sBgColor: "#FFFFFF",
    sColor: "#0066CC", sWmode: "transparent"}));
}
```

`sIFR.replaceElement` specifies a replacement rule that you want sIFR to apply. You can have as many of these as you like, each effecting a different type of element. The function takes a number of arguments that effect the display of the Flash replacement.

There are a few of these arguments, but the named ones you'll use most often are:

- **sSelector**

  sSelector is the CSS selector defining element(s) that you wish to replace. It uses a simplified CSS syntax, allowing you to select elements using the CSS selectors "#", ">", and ".", as well as the whitespace descendant selector. If you select multiple elements be sure to separate them with commas: ",".

- **sFlashSrc**

  sFlashSrc defines the location of the flash movie you want to use to replace the text. This file determines the font you'll be using for your Flash replacement.

- **sBGColor**

  sBGColor defines the background color you wish to use for the Flash replacement.

- **sColor**

  sColor defines the color of the text in the Flash replacement.

- **sWmode**

  sWmode defines the Window mode of the Flash replacement object. It allows you to set the transparency of the movie, and can be specified either as **transparent** or **opaque**. In **transparent** mode, **sBackgroundColor** will be ignored and the movie background will be transparent. In **opaque** mode the background color will be displayed. Some browsers have trouble displaying transparency; in such cases **sWmode** will fall back to the **opaque** mode. Just in case, make sure you set a background color even if you choose to use **transparent** mode, so that you won't be caught out in this situation.

You can supply to the function any of a number of other arguments, which will control everything from text transformation to alignment and padding. If you wish to read about them, the best place to look is in the documentation that comes with the sIFR package.

Once that replacement rule has been added to the end of the **sifr.js** file, it will perform that replacement when the page loads. Using the rule above, our page would look like Figure 1.14.

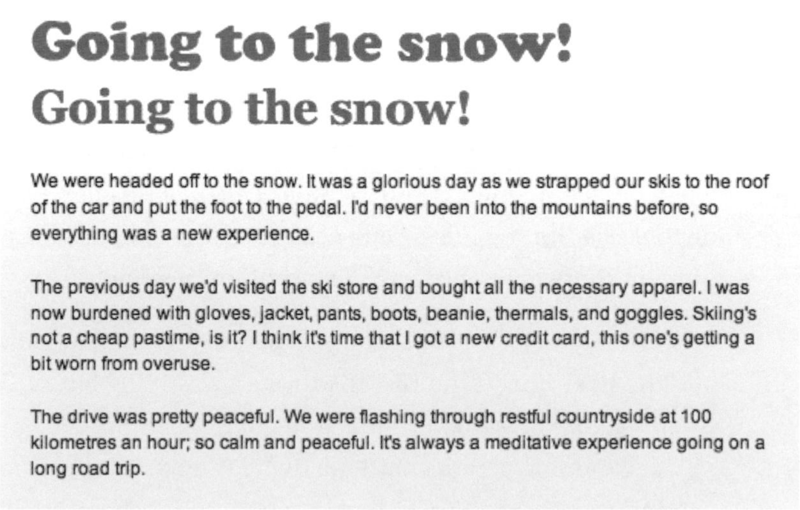

Going to the snow!
Going to the snow!

We were headed off to the snow. It was a glorious day as we strapped our skis to the roof of the car and put the foot to the pedal. I'd never been into the mountains before, so everything was a new experience.

The previous day we'd visited the ski store and bought all the necessary apparel. I was now burdened with gloves, jacket, pants, boots, beanie, thermals, and goggles. Skiing's not a cheap pastime, is it? I think it's time that I got a new credit card, this one's getting a bit worn from overuse.

The drive was pretty peaceful. We were flashing through restful countryside at 100 kilometres an hour; so calm and peaceful. It's always a meditative experience going on a long road trip.

Figure 1.14: Head of page after customized **sifr.js** file has been included

You'll notice that the heading is now shown twice. The upper display is the Flash replacement, the lower is the HTML text. They're both displayed simultaneously because we haven't yet included any of the special sIFR CSS.

Including the CSS

Inside the sIFR package is a CSS file called **sIFR-screen.css**, which we should include if we want the Flash replacement headings to display properly. This CSS hides any HTML text that has been replaced by Flash, so we don't see the double display as in Figure 1.14. Once we include this file, the page should look like Figure 1.15.

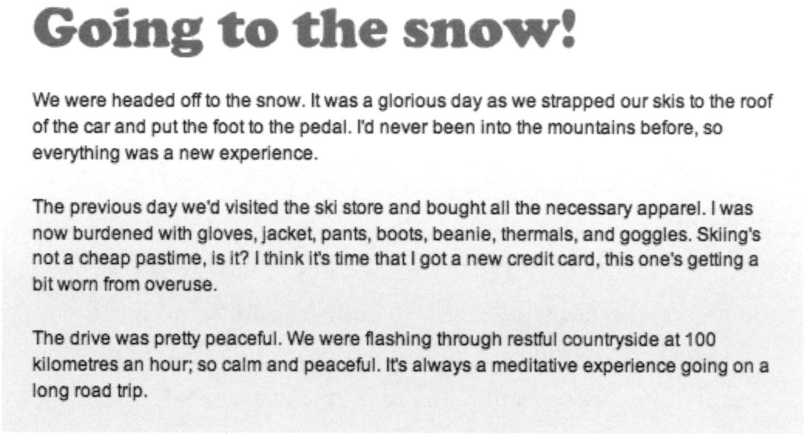

Figure 1.15: Page once **sIFR-screen.css** has been included

Tweaking the CSS

sIFR-screen.css, contains several default rules for **h1** to **h5** elements that help to determine the dimensions of the Flash replacements. In order to understand how you should use these rules, you need to understand how sIFR does its job and how fonts relate to one another.

You can see in Figure 1.14 that the Flash replacement and the HTML text are different lengths when displayed side by side. This discrepancy arises as a result of the fact that the font used in the Flash replacement differs from that used in the HTML, and because different fonts have different character metrics (including width, spacing, and so on).

This difference in length becomes a particular problem when a line of text starts to wrap onto the next line. If the HTML text isn't wrapping but the Flash text is, sIFR will shrink the size of the Flash text so that it fits onto one line. This means that the size of the Flash replacement may be inconsistent, depending upon the number of characters in the HTML text. Conversely, if the HTML text is wrapping when the Flash text isn't, then the sIFR will make the Flash characters really big in order to fill the space taken by two lines of HTML text. If the metrics of the Flash text don't match the metrics of the HTML text, the size of the Flash text will become variable for different character lengths. Compared with the previous figures, the Flash text in Figure 1.16 is smaller.

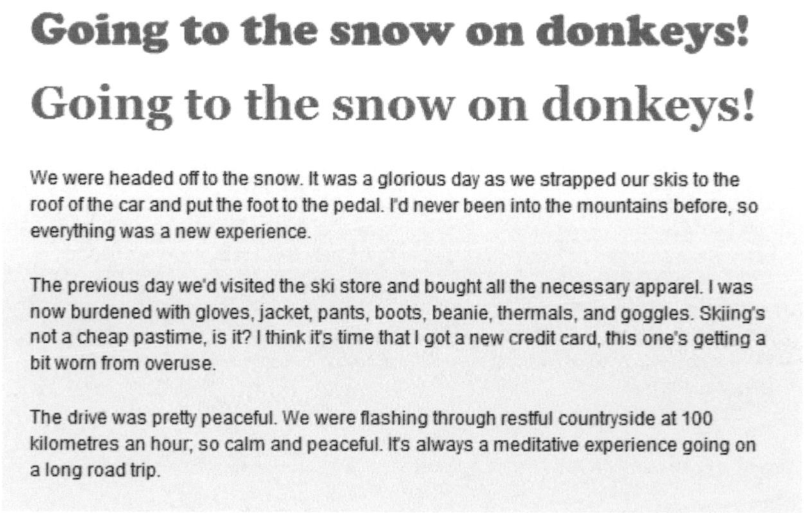

Going to the snow on donkeys!

Going to the snow on donkeys!

We were headed off to the snow. It was a glorious day as we strapped our skis to the roof of the car and put the foot to the pedal. I'd never been into the mountains before, so everything was a new experience.

The previous day we'd visited the ski store and bought all the necessary apparel. I was now burdened with gloves, jacket, pants, boots, beanie, thermals, and goggles. Skiing's not a cheap pastime, is it? I think it's time that I got a new credit card, this one's getting a bit worn from overuse.

The drive was pretty peaceful. We were flashing through restful countryside at 100 kilometres an hour; so calm and peaceful. It's always a meditative experience going on a long road trip.

Figure 1.16: sIFR text relative to space occupied by original HTML text

In order to let you pre-empt this potential problem, sIFR applies a class to the HTML element to let you know when Flash has been detected: sIFR-hasFlash.

You know that once this class has been applied the HTML text will be replaced by Flash, so you can tweak the text properties of the HTML to match the properties of the Flash text, achieving the same character heights, line-lengths, and so on.

In order to ensure our Cooper Black Flash text displays at the same length as our Georgia HTML text, we can modify the `letter-spacing`, giving the Georgia font a bit more space between characters to stretch it out:

> **TIP   Headings Side by Side**
>
> In order to see your tweaked HTML text alongside the Flash replacement, comment out the style near the top of **sIFR-screen.css** that applies to the sIFR-alternate class, like so:
>
> ```
> /*
> span.sIFR-alternate {
> …
> }
> */
> ```

```
.sIFR-hasFlash h1 {
  letter-spacing: 0.142em;
}
```

When you examine the comparison in Figure 1.17, you'll notice the heading lengths are almost identical:

Going to the snow!
Going to the snow!

We were headed off to the snow. It was a glorious day as we strapped our skis to the roof of the car and put the foot to the pedal. I'd never been into the mountains before, so everything was a new experience.

The previous day we'd visited the ski store and bought all the necessary apparel. I was now burdened with gloves, jacket, pants, boots, beanie, thermals, and goggles. Skiing's not a cheap pastime, is it? I think it's time that I got a new credit card, this one's getting a bit worn from overuse.

The drive was pretty peaceful. We were flashing through restful countryside at 100 kilometres an hour; so calm and peaceful. It's always a meditative experience going on a long road trip.

Figure 1.17: `letter-spacing` used to equalize metrics between Flash text and HTML text

As you can see in Figure 1.18, with proper metric adjustment of the HTML text, Flash replacement maintains consistent sizing through varying character lengths and multiple lines.

Going to the snow on donkeys!
Going to the snow on donkeys!

We were headed off to the snow. It was a glorious day as we strapped our skis to the roof of the car and put the foot to the pedal. I'd never been into the mountains before, so everything was a new experience.

The previous day we'd visited the ski store and bought all the necessary apparel. I was now burdened with gloves, jacket, pants, boots, beanie, thermals, and goggles. Skiing's not a cheap pastime, is it? I think it's time that I got a new credit card, this one's getting a bit worn from overuse.

The drive was pretty peaceful. We were flashing through restful countryside at 100 kilometres an hour; so calm and peaceful. It's always a meditative experience going on a long road trip.

Figure 1.18: The `letter-spacing` tweak maintaining sizing for varying character lengths

Once you've tweaked the metrics to cause the headings to appear exactly as you want, remember to add **visibility: hidden** to the rule, so that the user doesn't see the HTML text being distorted while the Flash replacement performs its calculation:

sIFR-screen.css (excerpt)

```
.sIFR-hasFlash h1 {
  visibility: hidden;
  letter-spacing: 0.142em;
}
```

After you've implemented all these changes for your particular font, you can sit back and relax. sIFR will now automatically change any **h1**s on your pages to Cooper Black without your having to lift a finger.

sIFR is superb for headings that require a unique typeface. However, it lacks the flexibility of image replacement. You can't distort the text, apply image masks, or make any other radical changes to the text beyond what Flash can normally do to text.

The other disadvantage to sIFR is that it can be a little resource-intensive. If you have a number of Flash-replaced headings on your page, the calculation time can weigh down page loading and affect the responsiveness of your interface. For that reason it's a good idea to use it sparingly and not apply it to large slabs of body text.

sIFR can also replace links, but you *do* lose some natural link functionality simply by way of the link being in Flash. Right-clicking the link won't bring up the normal browser context menu; mousing over the link won't indicate where it will lead. So, as with anything that could impact on usability, use sIFR carefully and with full knowledge of the consequences.

Summary

In this chapter, we've looked at the dual functions served by the seemingly humble heading: page hierarchy and identity. We've learned the various means by which we can circumvent the limitations placed upon our page design by the few typefaces available across most browsers, in order to ensure our pages stand out from the endless expanse of Arial or Times New Roman. We've discovered various types of image and Flash replacement—all techniques that allow unlimited creativity for heading design, but that require additional precautions by way of markup to display effectively for all users. We worked together through that markup to achieve the heading design we wanted, one that would work effectively in any user's browser.

Headings can certainly add that elusive uniqueness to your site that'll make it shine above the rest. As any good designer will tell you, beauty is in the detail—not only in the sense of how your headings strike the eye of the beholder, but how they actually function for all the different users who encounter your site. Not all browsers can handle your creative flights of CSS fancy, but there's ways around all sorts of browser limitations. By using the methods described in this chapter, you'll be able to add the most beautiful detail to any of your web pages, and ensure that they're accessible to any of your users.

2 Images

We've all heard it said that a picture tells a thousand words, and it's definitely one cliché that's endured for a reason. Images are a fantastic means of presenting information in ways that text cannot, which is why the marriage of web sites and images is a match made in heaven. From graphs and charts to photography and illustration, images are just as much a functional tool for the web designer as an aesthetic one.

In this chapter, we'll look at some of the most popular ways images are used on web sites. We'll work through the markup required for different manifestations of image galleries, for the design of web sites predominantly concerned with image presentation. We'll also learn about the issues of presentation and markup of contextual images, for sites that involve a combination of text and image.

As we'll see, there's more to images than meets the eye!

Photo Gallery

hotos » Album: Firenze, Italia 2006

the vase in the corner. This vase always intrigued me, in all its gaudiness. But I certainly did not wish to own it.

It is a big white vase painted with large pink, yellow, and purple flowers, butterflies, and ornamentation around the top. All the line work was painted in glossy, shiny gold. And all around the vase were three-dimensional figurines of cats attached on to it, so it would look like they were climbing the vase. The cats are cute, white, with gold-trimmed ears and tails.

The Cat Vase: The cats are cute, white, with gold-trimmed ears and tails.

Don't get me wrong. I love cats. But I was never one to collect memorabilia.

Years went by and I never put another thought to the vase. Then the day came that my father showed up to visit. He was holding the vase.

"Grandma told me to give this to you," he said with a smirk on his face.

"She did? But that was part of her will... Why is she giving it to me now?"

Image Galleries

Imagine that you have just walked into an art gallery. The pieces of art hang on well-lit expanses of white wall. There's ample spacing between the works, so that each has its own presence without any distraction from those adjacent. The rooms are very spacious and it's easy to find your way around the building. As you wander from room to room, you notice that within each of these rooms the works of art relate to each other. You know that, behind the scenes, a curator has put a lot of thought into the experience you have in this gallery while viewing the art.

A gallery web site should be conceptually similar to a real-life gallery such as this. You want to provide a clean, flexible space for your images to be displayed, with a corresponding sense of order and cohesion.

Creating an Image Page

The web page that displays your photograph, along with a title and possibly a description, is the equivalent of the expansive, blank walls in a real-life gallery.

Let's walk together through a basic example of how to create an image's page. We'll create the markup; add some style for the typography and colors of the images' titles and descriptions; style frames, margins, and layout; and provide the placement of the navigational thumbnails.

Building a Basic Example

As always, our image's page requires that we use well-structured markup:

photo.html (excerpt)

```
<!DOCTYPE html PUBLIC "-//W3C//DTD XHTML 1.0 Strict//EN"
    "http://www.w3.org/TR/xhtml1/DTD/xhtml1-strict.dtd">
<html xmlns="http://www.w3.org/1999/xhtml" xml:lang="en"
    lang="en">
<head>
<title>Photo Gallery</title>
<meta http-equiv="Content-Type" content="text/html;
    charset=utf-8" />
<link type="text/css" href="gallery.css" rel="stylesheet" />
</head>
<body>
<div id="content">
  <h1><a href="#">Photos</a> &raquo; <a href="#">Album:
      <em>Firenze, Italia 2006</em></a> &raquo;
      <em>Castello Il Palagio Orchard</em></h1>
```

```
   <p class="photo"><a href="#"><img alt="Photo: Castello Il
      Palagio Orchard" src="images/photo.jpg " /></a></p>
   <p class="description">A beautiful day for a wine-tasting and
      tour at <em>Castello Il Palagio</em> in Firenze, Italia.
   </p>
</div>
</body>
</html>
```

This example is fairly basic:

- The **h1** is acting as a title and a breadcrumb, in an effort to keep things really simple.
- The set name and image name are emphasized.
- The image is wrapped in a paragraph—which will make it easier to position and style— and links to a full-sized version. A **class** of **photo** is given to this paragraph for styling purposes.
- The description is a paragraph with a **class** of **description**.
- The photo, header, and description is wrapped in a **div** with an **id** of **content** for styling.
- Each image is no wider than 500px.
- Outside the **content div** is an unordered list used for a pagination-style navigation.

For your own implementation, the links' **href** values will need to be changed from **#** to their proper values. Our resulting page is shown in Figure 2.1.

Figure 2.1: The unstyled page

Adding Typography and Colors

Let's add some basic styles to our style sheet for the page's typography and colors, which will produce the result shown in Figure 2.2:

gallery.css (excerpt)

```
body {
  margin: 0;
  padding: 0;
  background-color: #fff;
  font: 62.5%/1.75em "Times New Roman", serif;
  color: #4d4d4d;
}
a:link, a {
  border-bottom: 1px dotted #960;
  text-decoration: none;
  color: #960;
}
a:hover {
  border-bottom: 1px solid #960;
}
```

Figure 2.2: Page showing basic styles

The colors and typefaces you choose should work well with the style of imagery you're using.

White is a great color for galleries because it's the most neutral color to work with, especially for a large variety of images, or for images that are changed frequently. On the downside, this means that you'll see the use of white everywhere on gallery sites, so you may want to think outside the square if uniqueness is a priority. I've seen some photo gallery web sites that use black or gray for their pages, and they look wonderful, but do be careful about crazier colors. Remember that the page colors you choose can really affect the mood of your images, and that rules of clean design should still apply. It's best to keep all design elements minimal: the visual focus of a gallery should be on the images.

I've chosen to use Times New Roman as it's clean and sophisticated without being a distraction from the images. Although sans serif typefaces are easier to read on-screen, our gallery uses very little text so the use of serif fonts won't be a problem.

Next, we style the **h1**, paragraphs (**p**) and unordered lists (**ul**) to display as in Figure 2.3:

gallery.css (excerpt)

```css
h1 {
  margin: 0 6px;
  padding: 0 0 .5em 0;
  font-style: italic;
  font-weight: normal;
  font-size: 1.25em;
  line-height: 2.375em;
  color: #ccc;
}
h1 em {
  color: #4d4d4d;
}
h1 a:link, h1 a, h1 a:hover, h1 a em, h1 a:link em,
    h1 a:hover em {
  border-color: #999;
  color: #999;
}
p, ul {
  margin: 0 6px;
  padding: 0;
}
```

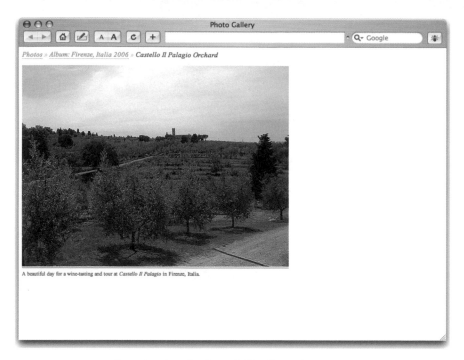

Figure 2.3: Page showing styled heading and paragraph

Styling the Images

Now, we'll style the image and the link that contains that image. For this example, we'll mimic a Polaroid-style photograph by using a white frame with a larger lower margin—a great place to add a date or copyright statement. To do this, we'll have an inset-style **border** around the image, and then an outset-style **border** around that, as shown in Figure 2.4. Here's the code:

gallery.css (excerpt)

```
img {
  display: block;
  margin: 0 auto 5px auto;
  border: 1px solid #ccc;
  border-bottom-color: #eee;
  border-left-color: #ddd;
  border-top-color: #bbb;
}
p.photo {
  margin: 0 0 10px 0;
  float: left;
  width: 75%;
  text-align: center;
  background-color: #fff;
  line-height: 1em;
}
```

```
p.photo a {
  display: block;
  float: left;
  margin: 0;
  padding: 4px 4px 9px 4px;
  border: 1px solid #ccc;
  border-top-color: #eee;
  border-right-color: #ddd;
  border-bottom-color: #bbb;
  background-color: #fff;
  text-align: center;
}
p.photo a:hover {
  border-color: #ccc;
  background-color: #eee;
}
p.description {
  clear: left;
}
```

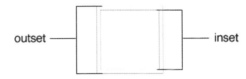

Figure 2.4: Example of an inset and an outset border

The definition of separate colors for each side gives the **border** on the image the desired inset look. We could have used the **inset border-style** that CSS already provides, but the colors for the light and dark borders differ between browsers.

To create the look we want, we use a 1px, solid **border**, and specify **#ccc** as its color. We use a slightly lighter shade (**#ddd**) for the right **border**, and darker shades for the top (**#bbb**) and left (**#eee**) **border**s. The result fools the eye into seeing a three-dimensional edge.

The addition of a 5px **margin** to the lower edge distances the outside border from the image. It's aesthetically pleasing to have a larger space on the bottom than around the sides, and it works well with the Polaroid-style look we're trying to create.

The link that contains the image has a solid border of 1px, which uses the same colors as before, although they're reversed to create an "outset" look (we've switched the top and bottom colors, and the left and right colors). We also add a **padding** of 4px. This **padding**, plus the 1px **border** we've added to the image and the 1px border we've applied to the link, provides us with the 6px value that we've applied for the **h1**'s and paragraph's **margin**s, and helps the edge of the text line up with the image, instead of the outside border.

To ensure that the outside border that's applied to the link containing the image snaps snug to that image, we float the paragraph and link to the left, and apply a **75% width** to the paragraph. This **width** is a workaround that was developed for Internet Explorer to avoid the outside **border** filling the entire width of the page in that browser; the page still renders as expected in other browsers.

Next we'll add some hover styles: a subtle, light gray **background**, and one color for the **border** for all four sides. The **description** paragraph is then set to **clear: left**, to clear the float from the above-image paragraph. The result is shown in Figure 2.5.

Figure 2.5: Page showing the bordered image

Producing a Quick and Simple Layout

Now, we want to define the spacing and **width** of the **div** that contains all the elements of our page. We'll also increase the font size for items within this **div**, to create the effect shown in Figure 2.6. By adding the code at this point, instead of at the **body** level, we ensure that relative **padding** and **margin** sizes are affected only within this **div**:

```
                                                              gallery.css (excerpt)
#content {
  margin: 0 auto 20px 20px;
  padding: 1em 0 0 0;
  width: 512px;
  background-color:#fff;
  font-size: 1.25em;
  line-height: 1.75em;
}
```

Because the images we're using are no wider than 500px, and we want to have room for the **border** around each image, we'll use a **width** of **512px** for **#content**. You can vary this value to reflect the maximum width of your images. I recommend setting a maximum of 500px to ensure that the entire image will fit within most browser viewports. Just make sure that the **width** of **#content** is equal to the total **width** of the image plus any left or right **padding** and **border** properties.

Figure 2.6: Page showing the styled **div**

We're almost done!

Styling the Pagination Thumbnails

Now that the basic layout of the photo, title, and description has been created, we'll style the navigational thumbnails that will appear to the right of the main image on each page. These images will provide a view of the previous and next images in our gallery.

After the closing **div** for **#content**, add the following markup:

photo.html (excerpt)

```
<ul class="navigation thumbnails">
  <li><a href="#"><img src="images/thumb1.jpg" alt="Thumb:
      Graffiti" /><br />&laquo; Graffiti</a></li>
  <li><a href="#"><img src="images/thumb3.jpg" alt="Thumb: Ponte
      Vecchio" /><br />Ponte Vecchio &raquo;</a></li>
</ul>
```

Again, you'll need to change the **href** attributes from **#** to link to their proper locations.

On some of the pages we'll be creating, the navigation won't include images, but it does on this page. Let's take advantage of the fact that we're able to use two classes, and apply a **navigation** class to all instances of this pagination-style navigation. We'll use the **thumbnails** class only for unordered lists that contain thumbnail images—we'll meet **thumbnails** again when we create our thumbnail page.

Both the image and the text are wrapped in the same link, because we want the title of the image to appear underneath the image, but to share the same link, so that the hover effects will be the same for both elements. The linebreak (**br**) is not required, but we add this so that the title will continue to appear beneath the image when the page is viewed unstyled.

> **NOTE   *Using a Non-breaking Space***
>
> We're using a left-angled quote («) and a right-angled quote (») as design elements to provide "previous page" and "next page" navigation. In the event that the title wraps, we don't want these symbols to end up on separate lines, which is why we used a non-breaking space (** **).

As you can see in Figure 2.7, the linebreak adds an unsightly amount of space between the thumbnail and the title. We can take care of that problem simply by setting the **br** to **display: none**. The image is already set to **display: block**, so the title will display on its own line beneath the image, as intended.

Figure 2.7: Page showing thumbnail navigation

gallery.css (excerpt)

```
br {
  display: none;
}
```

Next, we'll make the thumbnails appear in a style that's similar to the main image, by making them share some of the same styles. Then we'll position the thumbnails to the right of the page:

gallery.css (excerpt)

```
ul.navigation {
  margin: 0 0 10px 0;
  padding: 0;
  float: left;
  text-align: center;
  background-color: #fff;
  line-height: 1em;
  list-style: none;
  position: absolute;
  top: 58px;
  left: 550px;
}
```

As you can see, these are very similar to the **p.photo** styles, but for a few minor differences:

- The **padding** needs to be set to **0**.
- We don't need to set a **width**.
- We turn the bullets off using **list-style: none;**.
- The **navigation ul** is positioned to the right of the main image.

Next, we need to style the list items (**li**):

gallery.css (excerpt)

```
ul.navigation li {
  display: inline;
  margin: 0;
  padding: 0;
}
```

Now, we'll style the thumbnail images. Since the thumbnails will look exactly like the main photo, we can just add these new, thumbnail-specific styles to the existing styles we have for **p.photo a** and **p.photo a:hover**, like so:

gallery.css (excerpt)

```
p.photo a, ul.thumbnails a {
  display: block;
  float: left;
  margin: 0;
  padding: 4px 4px 9px 4px;
  border: 1px solid #ccc;
  border-top-color: #eee;
  border-right-color: #ddd;
  border-bottom-color: #bbb;
  background-color: #fff;
  text-align: center;
}
p.photo a:hover, ul.thumbnails a:hover {
  border-color: #ccc;
  background-color: #eee;
}
```

Next, we need to add a **width** and a right **margin**, which will need to be created as a separate style rule, since **p.photo** won't use it:

gallery.css (excerpt)

```
ul.thumbnails a {
  width: 80px;
  margin-right: 10px;
  margin-bottom: 10px;
}
```

The thumbnail images we used have 75x75px dimensions, so we're using an 80px `width` value here. The result of our efforts is shown in Figure 2.8.

Figure 2.8: Page showing styled thumbnail navigation

NOTE   *Considering the Portrait Photo*

When you're creating a gallery page, it's always important to consider alternate formats; make sure that your page still looks nice when a portrait (or vertical) photograph is used. Try to avoid chopping off any portion of your image, as has occurred in Figure 2.9. Unfortunately, this scenario is often unavoidable when using portrait images; you'll just need to weigh up the cropping of an image against having your users scroll down to see it all.

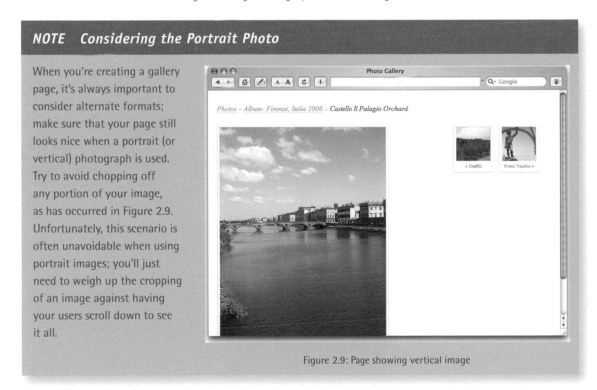

Figure 2.9: Page showing vertical image

You now have a basic image page for your gallery. But how are visitors enticed to view this image page in the first place? By seeing the associated thumbnails page, of course!

Creating a Thumbnails Page

We'll create a typical thumbnails page—a display of small images, each of which links to its respective image page. Actually, since we've already created the look and feel of the image page, most of the groundwork is completed. The markup for our thumbnails page looks like this:

thumbnails.html

```
<!DOCTYPE html PUBLIC "-//W3C//DTD XHTML 1.0 Strict//EN"
"http://www.w3.org/TR/xhtml1/DTD/xhtml1-strict.dtd">
<html xmlns="http://www.w3.org/1999/xhtml" xml:lang="en"
   lang="en">
<head>
  <title>Photo Gallery</title>
  <meta http-equiv="Content-Type" content="text/html;
     charset=utf-8" />
  <link type="text/css" href="gallery.css" rel="stylesheet" />
</head>
<body>
  <div id="content">
    <h1><a href="/">Photos</a> &raquo; Album: <em>Firenze,
       Italia 2006</em></h1>
    <ul class="thumbnails">
      <li><a href="#"><img alt="Thumb"
         src="images/thumb1.jpg" /></a></li>
      <li><a href="#"><img alt="Thumb"
         src="images/thumb2.jpg" /></a></li>
      <li><a href="#"><img alt="Thumb"
         src="images/thumb3.jpg" /></a></li>
      <li><a href="#"><img alt="Thumb"
         src="images/thumb4.jpg" /></a></li>
      <li><a href="#"><img alt="Thumb"
         src="images/thumb5.jpg" /></a></li>
      <li><a href="#"><img alt="Thumb"
         src="images/thumb6.jpg" /></a></li>
      <li><a href="#"><img alt="Thumb"
         src="images/thumb7.jpg" /></a></li>
      <li><a href="#"><img alt="Thumb"
         src="images/thumb8.jpg" /></a></li>
      <li><a href="#"><img alt="Thumb"
         src="images/thumb9.jpg" /></a></li>
      <li><a href="#"><img alt="Thumb"
         src="images/thumb10.jpg" /></a></li>
      <li><a href="#"><img alt="Thumb"
```

```
         src="images/thumb11.jpg" /></a></li>
      <li><a href="#"><img alt="Thumb"
         src="images/thumb12.jpg" /></a></li>
      <li><a href="#"><img alt="Thumb"
         src="images/thumb13.jpg" /></a></li>
      <li><a href="#"><img alt="Thumb"
         src="images/thumb14.jpg" /></a></li>
      <li><a href="#"><img alt="Thumb"
         src="images/thumb15.jpg" /></a></li>
      <li><a href="#"><img alt="Thumb"
         src="images/thumb16.jpg" /></a></li>
      <li><a href="#"><img alt="Thumb"
         src="images/thumb17.jpg" /></a></li>
      <li><a href="#"><img alt="Thumb"
         src="images/thumb18.jpg" /></a></li>
      <li><a href="#"><img alt="Thumb"
         src="images/thumb19.jpg" /></a></li>
      <li><a href="#"><img alt="Thumb"
         src="images/thumb20.jpg" /></a></li>
      <li><a href="#"><img alt="Thumb"
         src="images/thumb21.jpg" /></a></li>
      <li><a href="#"><img alt="Thumb"
         src="images/thumb22.jpg" /></a></li>
      <li><a href="#"><img alt="Thumb"
         src="images/thumb23.jpg" /></a></li>
      <li><a href="#"><img alt="Thumb"
         src="images/thumb24.jpg" /></a></li>
      <li><a href="#"><img alt="Thumb"
         src="images/thumb25.jpg" /></a></li>
    </ul>
  </div>
  <ul class="navigation">
    <li><a href="#">&laquo; Previous</a></li>
    <li><a href="#">Next &raquo;</a></li>
  </ul>
 </body>
</html>
```

You'll notice that this markup is very similar to the image page's markup, except the **h1** is different, and the description area has been removed. We've created an unordered list to contain the thumbnails; it utilizes the **class** of **thumbnails** that we used previously on the navigation for the photo page.

The number of thumbnails displayed on this page can be varied to suit your preferences. I've chosen to display 25, as the layout is wide enough to accommodate five thumbnails per row and per column, which echoes the 1:1 proportions of the thumbnails themselves. A little aesthetically pleasing balance is never a bad thing!

The pagination-style navigation is very similar to the navigation on our single image page, but the **class** of **thumbnails** was removed, since these links don't contain thumbnail images and don't need to be styled as such. At the moment, our page appears as in Figure 2.10.

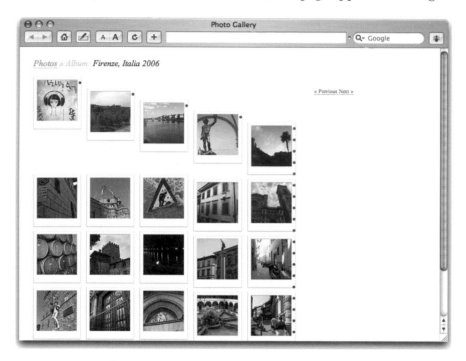

Figure 2.10: The thumbnails page before additional styling

Styling the Thumbnails

To produce the display shown in Figure 2.11, we now need to add the following styles for **thumbnails**:

```
                                                          gallery.css (excerpt)

ul.thumbnails {
  margin: 0 0 10px 0;
  padding: 0;
  float: left;
  text-align: center;
  background-color: #fff;
  line-height: 1em;
  list-style: none;
}
```

These styles are the same as those we used for **navigation**, except that we're not positioning this unordered list. We also want to style the list items in exactly the same way as we did for the **navigation** list items. The results of this markup are shown in Figure 2.11:

```
                                                        gallery.css (excerpt)
ul.thumbnails li, ul.navigation li {
  display: inline;
  margin: 0;
  padding: 0;
}
```

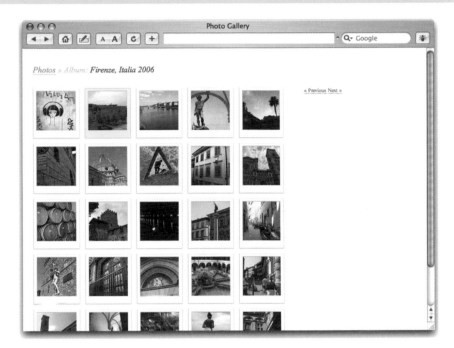

Figure 2.11: Thumbnails page showing styled thumbnails

Finally, let's style the navigation. As we're not using a thumbnail image, we can use a slightly different style in this case:

```
                                                        gallery.css (excerpt)
ul.navigation a {
  display: block;
  float: left;
  margin: 0 10px 10px 0;
  padding: 4px 4px 6px 4px;
  border: 0;
  background-color: #fff;
  text-align: center;
  width: 80px;
}
ul.navigation a:hover {
  background-color: #eee;
  border: 0;
}
```

The **navigation** styling differs from the **thumbnails** styles, in that a smaller `padding` value is applied to the bottom, and there is no `border` on the links.

Make sure that this styling comes before the `ul.thumbnails` styles in your markup so that the `borders` and `padding` display correctly, as they do in Figure 2.12.

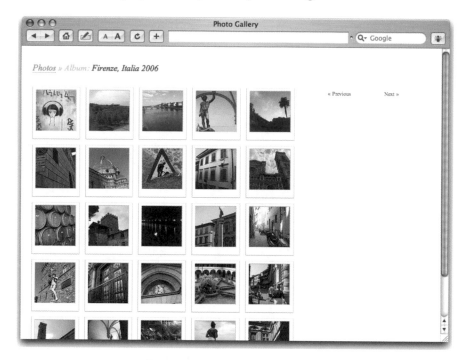

Figure 2.12: Completed thumbnails page

Congratulations—you now have a thumbnails page and an image page. All we need to do now is make an album page.

Creating an Album Page

If you have a lot of images, you probably want to categorize them into albums. And if you have a lot of albums, it's best to give the viewer more information than a simple list of the albums' titles. With the new page we'll create in this section, your visitors should be able to gain a good idea of what each of your albums contains.

Some information that can be included on the album page includes:

- a brief description of the album
- the number of photographs in that album
- a carefully selected thumbnail that represents the album

Looking at an Example

Once again, the basic groundwork has already been done. Here's the markup:

albums.html

```
<!DOCTYPE html PUBLIC "-//W3C//DTD XHTML 1.0 Strict//EN"
"http://www.w3.org/TR/xhtml1/DTD/xhtml1-strict.dtd">
<html xmlns="http://www.w3.org/1999/xhtml" xml:lang="en"
   lang="en">
<head>
  <title>Photo Gallery</title>
  <meta http-equiv="Content-Type" content="text/html;
     charset=utf-8" />
  <link type="text/css" href="gallery.css" rel="stylesheet" />
</head>
<body>
  <div id="content">
    <h1><em>Photos</em></h1>
    <h2><a href="#">Firenze, Italia 2006</a></h2>
    <p class="thumb"><a href="#"><img alt="Thumbnail: Firenze,
       Italia 2006" src="images/thumb1.jpg" /><br />259
       Photos</a></p>
    <p>Living in Firenze, Italia {Florence, Italy} for
       one month. This is the highlight of my life.</p>
    <h2><a href="#">Boston, Massachusetts 2006</a></h2>
    <p class="thumb"><a href="#">
      <img alt="" src="images/thumb26.jpg" />
    <br />38 Photos</a></p>
    <p>From my business trip to Boston {May 2006} when Vineet
       &amp; I were working on Mass.gov.</p>
    <h2><a href="#">Barcelona, Espa&ntilde;a 2006</a></h2>
    <p class="thumb"><a href="#"><img alt=""
       src="images/thumb27.jpg" /><br />110 Photos</a></p>
    <p>My first venture into Europe &amp; a wonderful week of
       great food, art, architecture, &amp; culture.</p>
  </div>
  <ul class="navigation">
    <li><a href="#">&laquo; Previous 3 Sets </a></li>
    <li><a href="#">Next 3 Sets &raquo;</a></li>
  </ul>
</body>
</html>
```

Obviously, the number of albums displayed on the page can vary, but I suggest you keep the number under ten to prevent visual clutter. In the example shown in Figure 2.13, we've used three. We've applied a **class** of **thumb** to the paragraph holding the thumbnail image. The total number of photos in each album appears underneath that album's thumbnail image, similar to the display of the pagination thumbnails used on the image page. An **h2** has been added to hold the album titles, and a paragraph is used for the descriptions.

Figure 2.13: The album page, without additional styles applied

Styling the Album Page

We're almost done! We just need to style the **h2**s and the thumbnails. Here, the **h2** is styled to look and behave similarly to the images, with the same hover effects. We add `clear: left;` to the **h2** to ensure that each new album clears the floated thumbnail of the album that precedes it:

```
h2 {
  margin: 0 0 5px 0;
  font-weight: normal;
  font-size: 1.5em;
  text-align: left;
  clear: left;
}
h2 a:link, h2 a {
  display: block;
  padding: 0 5px;
  border: 1px solid #ccc;
  border-top-color: #eee;
  border-right-color: #ddd;
  border-bottom-color: #bbb;
```

```
}
h2 a:hover {
  border-color: #ccc;
  background-color: #eee;
}
```

Finally, we'll style the thumbnails to appear like those in Figure 2.14, which share some styles with **ul.thumbnails**.

```
p.thumb, ul.thumbnails {
  margin: 0 0 10px 0;
  padding: 0;
  float: left;
  text-align: center;
  background-color: #fff;
  line-height: 1em;
  list-style: none;
}
p.photo a, p.thumb a, ul.thumbnails a {
  display: block;
  float: left;
  margin: 0;
  padding: 4px 4px 9px 4px;
  border: 1px solid #ccc;
  border-top-color: #eee;
  border-right-color: #ddd;
  border-bottom-color: #bbb;
  background-color: #fff;
  text-align: center;
}
p.thumb a, ul.thumbnails a {
  width: 80px;
  margin-right: 10px;
  margin-bottom: 10px;
}
p.photo a:hover, p.thumb a:hover, ul.thumbnails a:hover {
  border: 1px solid #ccc;
  background-color: #eee;
}
```

Figure 2.14: The album page displaying additional styles

Here's what the final style sheet should look like; it can be used on all three pages:

gallery.css

```
body {
  margin: 0;
  padding: 0;
  background-color: #fff;
  font: 62.5%/1.75em "Times New Roman", serif;
  color: #4d4d4d;
}
a:link, a {
  border-bottom:1px dotted #960;
  color: #960;
  text-decoration: none;
}
a:hover {
  border-bottom:1px solid #960;
}
h1 {
  margin: 05 6px;
  padding: 0 0 .5em 0;
  font-style: italic;
  font-weight: normal;
  font-size: 1.25em;
  line-height: 2.375em;
  color: #ccc;
}
```

```css
h1 em {
  color: #4d4d4d;
}
h1 a:link, h1 a, h1 a:hover, h1 a em, h1 a:link em,
    h1 a:hover em {
  border-color: #999;
  color: #999;
}
h2 {
  margin: 0 0 5px 0;
  font-weight: normal;
  font-size: 1.5em;
  text-align: left;
  clear: left;
}
h2 a:link, h2 a {
  display: block;
  padding: 0 5px;
  border: 1px solid #ccc;
  border-top-color: #eee;
  border-right-color: #ddd;
  border-bottom-color: #bbb;
}
h2 a:hover {
  border-color: #ccc;
  background-color: #eee;
}
p, ul {
  margin: 0 6px;
  padding: 0;
}
img {
  display: block;
  margin: 0 auto 5px auto;
  border:1px solid #ccc;
  border-bottom-color: #eee;
  border-left-color: #ddd;
  border-top-color: #bbb;
}
br {
  display: none;
}
#content {
  margin: 0 auto 20px 20px;
  padding: 1em 0 0 0;
  width: 512px;
  background-color: #fff;
  font-size: 1.25em;
  line-height: 1.75em;
```

```
p.photo {
  margin: 0 0 10px 0;
  float: left;
  width: 75%;
  text-align: center;
  background-color: #fff;
  line-height: 1em;
}
ul.navigation {
  margin: 0 0 10px 0;
  padding: 0;
  float: left;
  text-align: center;
  background-color: #fff;
  line-height: 1em;
  list-style: none;
  position: absolute;
  top: 76px;
  left: 550px;
}
p.thumb, ul.thumbnails {
  margin: 0 0 10px 0;
  padding: 0;
  float: left;
  text-align: center;
  background-color: #fff;
  line-height: 1em;
  list-style: none;
}
ul.thumbnails li, ul.navigation li {
  display: inline;
  margin: 0;
  padding: 0;
}
ul.navigation a {
  display: block;
  float: left;
  margin: 0 10px 10px 0;
  padding: 4px 4px 6px 4px;
  border: 0;
  background-color: #fff;
  text-align: center;
  width: 80px;
}
```

```
p.photo a, p.thumb a, ul.thumbnails a {
  display: block;
  float: left;
  margin: 0;
  padding: 4px 4px 9px 4px;
  border: 1px solid #ccc;
  border-top-color: #eee;
  border-right-color: #ddd;
  border-bottom-color: #bbb;
  background-color: #fff;
  text-align: center;
}
p.thumb a, ul.thumbnails a {
  width: 80px;
  margin-right: 10px;
  margin-bottom: 10px;
}
ul.navigation a:hover {
  background-color: #eee;
  border: 0;
}
p.photo a:hover, p.thumb a:hover, ul.thumbnails a:hover {
  border: 1px solid #ccc;
  background-color: #eee;
}
p.description {
  clear: left;
}
```

We've finished marking up and styling our experimental image page, thumbnails, and album list, and we have a clean, simple image gallery! At the end of this chapter, in Further Resources, you'll find a list of some great examples of online image galleries, along with a couple of gallery and photo album resources.

Contextual Images

Contextual images usually appear in news articles or weblog entries, where they provide additional visual information or help to illustrate the content. Sometimes they're used in a masthead-like manner to introduce the content. Other times, contextual images may be embedded throughout the content, the text wrapping around them. They may also be accompanied by a descriptive caption.

This section shows some of the interesting ways in which contextual images can be displayed, and provides the markup necessary to achieve these effects.

Placing Introductory Images

Introductory images are most typically seen on designers' weblogs, as shown in Figure 2.15, but these images are a fun way for anyone to introduce a post.

As the name suggests, introductory images appear at the beginning of the text. However, you can give them a lot more impact by playing around with their placement via the manipulation of their borders and padding values.

Figure 2.15: Introductory image used at Binary Bonsai

Using Borders and Padding

Let's work through an example, which you can see in Figure 2.16, that uses borders and padding to extend an image beyond the width of the page content. This approach makes the layout a little more interesting, and makes the image seem more deliberate—it doesn't seem as if it's just been "placed" there.

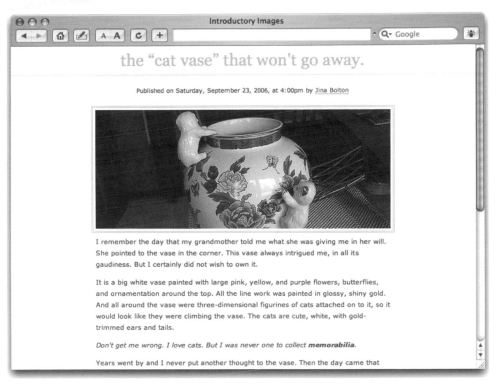

Figure 2.16: Introductory photo using borders and padding

It's very easy to create this look. We start with the proper markup—simply replace the text and images used here with the content that you want:

intro-image.html (excerpt)

```
<!DOCTYPE html PUBLIC "-//W3C//DTD XHTML 1.1//EN"
"http://www.w3.org/TR/xhtml11/DTD/xhtml11.dtd">
<html xmlns="http://www.w3.org/1999/xhtml">
<head>
  <meta http-equiv="Content-Type" content="text/html;
    charset=UTF-8" />
  <link type="text/css" href="intro-image.css" rel="stylesheet"
    />
  <title>Introductory Images</title>
</head>
<body>
  <h1>The &ldquo;Cat Vase&rdquo; that won't go away.</h1>
  <p><cite>Published on Saturday, September 23, 2006, at 4:00pm
    by <a href="# ">Jina Bolton</a></cite></p>
  <div id="content">
    <img src="images/intro-photo.jpg" class="intro" alt="The Cat
      Vase" />
```

```
      <p>I remember the day that my grandmother told me what she
         was giving me in her will. She pointed to the vase in
         corner. This vase always intrigued me, in all its
         gance and gaudiness. But I certainly did not wish to
         it.</p>
         is a big white vase painted with large pink, yellow,
         purple flowers, butterflies, and ornamentation
         ound the top. All the line work was painted in glossy,
         iny gold. And all around the vase were
         ree-dimensional figurines of cats attached on to it,
         it would look like they were climbing the vase.
         he cats are cute, white, with gold-trimmed ears and
         tails.</p>
      <p><em>Don't get me wrong. I love cats. But I was never one
         to collect <strong>memorabilia</strong>.</em></p>
      <p>Years went by and I never put another thought to the vase.
         Then the day came that my father showed up to visit.
         He was holding the vase.</p>
      <p>&quot;Grandma told me to give this to you,&quot; he said
         with a smirk on his face.</p>
      <p>&quot;She did? But that was part of her will... Why is she
         giving it to me now?&quot;</p>
      <p>&quot;Guess she wanted to get rid of it.&quot;</p>
      <p>I reluctantly received the vase. I kept it in the closet
         of my old bedroom I had when I lived with my boyfriend
         at the time. After I moved out into my own apartment,
         I didn't think much of it again. About a year went by,
         and I was moving once again to a nicer apartment. My
         ex-boyfriend began bringing things that I had left at
         his house. I didn't realize how much I had left over
         there.</p>
      <p>Then the day came that Michael showed up at the door.
         He was holding the vase, in a much similar style that
         my father had done, with the same smirk.</p>
      <p>I don't know what to do with it. My grandmother told
         me she paid $200 for it, so I don't want to just get
         rid of it. It's definitely not my style, and certainly
         doesn't match anything in my home. But at the same time,
         it's almost too funny to get rid of. I mean, how often
         do you see a vase this ornamental and bizarre?</p>
      <p>I've considered maybe putting it on eBay but I think I
         might hold on to it just for a little while longer.
         It's certainly photogenic. </p>
   </div>
  </body>
  </html>
```

The content and image are contained within a **div** with a **class** of **content**, and we've applied a **class** of **intro** to the image. The result is shown in Figure 2.17.

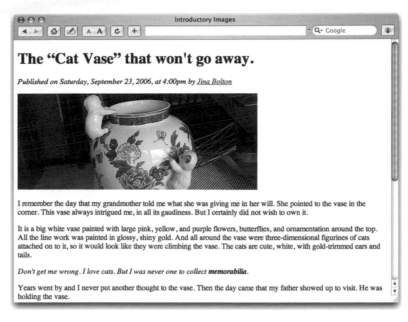

Figure 2.17: The unstyled introductory photo

Now, we'll style the page's typography, and apply the colors for its background, border, and font. These styles are merely applied for the sake of the page design, and are not required by the introductory image itself:

intro-image.css (excerpt)

```
body {
  margin: 0;
  padding: 0;
  background-color: #fff;
  font: 62.5%/1.75em "Trebuchet MS", Verdana, sans-serif;
  text-align: center;
  color: #4d4d4d;
}
#content {
  margin: 0 auto;
  padding: 1em 0;
  width: 500px;
  background-color:#fff;
  font-size: 1.125em;
  line-height: 1.75em;
  text-align: left;
}
a:link, a {
  border-bottom:1px dotted #960;
  color: #960;
  text-decoration: none;
}
```

```
h1 {
  margin: 0;
  padding: 0;
  border-bottom: 3px solid #eee;
  font: 2.75em/1.75em Georgia, serif;
  text-align: center;
  text-transform: lowercase;
  color: #cc6;
}
p {
  margin: 0;
  padding: 0 0 1em 0;
}
cite {
  display: block;
  margin-top: 2em;
  font-style: normal;
  font-size: 1em;
  line-height: 1em;
  text-align: center;
}
```

Now, we style the image. We'll add 4px of **padding**, and a 3px **border** with a **double** style, so that the image has what appears to be two **border**s surrounding it:

intro-image.css (excerpt)

```
img.intro {
  padding: 4px;
  border:3px double #ccc;
  background-color: #fff;
  margin:0 -7px;
}
```

The container is 500px wide, so the text stays within those boundaries. The image is also 500px wide, but since we've applied **padding** and **border** properties to it as well, we need to compensate for them. Due to the 4px **padding** and 3px **border**, our **intro** image needs to have a negative **margin** of 7px on the left and right to allow the **border** properties to extend beyond the **#content div**. The **padding** and **border** properties can be adjusted to suit your taste; just make sure that the negative **margin** is the same as the total of your **padding** and **border** properties.

In Figure 2.18, we see an image that's 500px wide—the same as the content area.

I remember the day that my grandmother told me what she was giving me in her will. She pointed to the vase in the corner. This vase always intrigued me, in all its

Figure 2.18: Styled introductory image

Styling Images and Captions

If you look at a news-related web site, you'll see that the images that illustrate the articles are often accompanied by captions. The caption is most commonly found beneath or beside the image, as shown in Figure 2.19.

We'll start, once again, with a page of semantic markup:

The Cat Vase: The cats are cute, white, with gold-trimmed ears and tails.

Figure 2.19: Basic image captioning

captions-1a.html (excerpt)

```
<!DOCTYPE html PUBLIC "-//W3C//DTD XHTML 1.1//EN"
    "http://www.w3.org/TR/xhtml11/DTD/xhtml11.dtd">
<html xmlns="http://www.w3.org/1999/xhtml">
<head>
  <meta http-equiv="Content-Type" content="text/html;
      charset=UTF-8" />
  <link type="text/css" rel="stylesheet" href="captions-1a.css" />
  <title>Images &amp; Captions</title>
</head>
<body>
  <div id="page">
    <h1>The &ldquo;Cat Vase&rdquo; that won't go away.</h1>
    <p><cite>Published on Saturday, September 23, 2006, at
        4:00pm by <a href="#">Jina Bolton</a></cite></p>
    <div id="content">
      <div class="captioned_photo">
        <img src="images/captions-1.jpg" alt="Cat Vase!" />
        <p><span><strong>The Cat Vase:</strong> The cats are
            cute, white, with gold-trimmed ears and tails.
            </span></p>
      </div>
```

```
<p>I remember the day that my grandmother told me what she
   was giving me in her will. She pointed to the vase in
   the corner. This vase always intrigued me, in all its
   gaudiness. But I certainly did not wish to own it.</p>
<p>It is a big white vase painted with large pink, yellow,
   and purple flowers, butterflies, and ornamentation
   around the top. All the line work was painted in
   glossy, shiny gold. And all around the vase were
   three-dimensional figurines of cats attached on to it,
   so it would look like they were climbing the vase.
   The cats are cute, white, with gold-trimmed ears and
   tails.</p>
<p><em>Don't get me wrong. I love cats. But I was never
   one to collect <strong>memorabilia</strong>.</em></p>
<p>Years went by and I never put another thought to the
   vase. Then the day came that my father showed up to
   visit. He was holding the vase.</p>
<p>&quot;Grandma told me to give this to you,&quot; he
   said with a smirk on his face.</p>
<p>&quot;She did? But that was part of her will... Why
   is she giving it to me now?&quot;</p>
<p>&quot;Guess she wanted to get rid of it.&quot;</p>
<p>I reluctantly received the vase. I kept it in the
   closet of my old bedroom I had when I lived with my
   boyfriend at the time. After I moved out into my own
   apartment, I didn't think much of it again. About a
   year went by, and I was moving once again to a nicer
   apartment. My ex-boyfriend began bringing things that
   I had left at his house. I didn't realize how much I
   had left over there.</p>
<p>Then the day came that Michael showed up at the door.
   He was holding the vase, in a much similar style that
   my father had done, with the same smirk.</p>
<p>I don't know what to do with it. My grandmother told
   me she paid $200 for it, so I don't want to just get
   rid of it. It's definitely not my style, and certainly
   doesn't match anything in my home. But at the same
   time, it's almost too funny to get rid of. I mean, how
   often do you see a vase this ornamental and bizarre?</p>
<p>I've considered maybe putting it on eBay but I think I
   might hold on to it just for a little while longer.
   It's certainly photogenic. </p>
    </div>
  </div>
</body>
</html>
```

We've wrapped both the image and the caption in a `div` with a `class` of **captioned_photo**, and have also applied a `span`, which we'll use for styling purposes later on. Now, let's add some basic page styles:

```
                                                  captions-1a.css (excerpt)

body {
  margin: 0;
  padding: 0;
  background-color: #fff;
  font: 62.5%/1.75em Verdana, sans-serif;
  text-align: center;
  color: #4d4d4d;
}
#page {
  margin: 0 auto;
  width: 75%;
  text-align: left;
}
#content {
  padding: 1em;
  font: 1.25em/1.75em "Times New Roman", serif
}
a:link, a {
  border-bottom:1px dotted #369;
  color: #369;
  text-decoration: none;
}
a:hover {
  border-bottom:1px solid #369;
}
h1 {
  margin: 0;
  padding: 0;
  border-bottom: 3px double #ccc;
  font: 3em/1.75em "Times New Roman", serif;
  font-variant: small-caps;
  letter-spacing:-.05em;
  text-align: center;
  color: #999;
}
```

```
h2 {
  margin: 2em 0 1em 0;
  padding: 0;
  border-top: 1px solid #ccc;
  border-bottom: 3px double #eee;
  font-style: italic;
  font-weight: normal;
  font-size: 1.25em;
  line-height: 1.75em;
}
p {
  margin: 0;
  padding: 0 0 1em 0;
}
cite {
  display: block;
  margin-top: 1.25em;
  font: normal normal 1em/1.75em Verdana, sans-serif;
  text-align: center;
}
```

The result of this markup is depicted in Figure 2.20.

Figure 2.20: Page displaying without image caption styles

Let's now style the photos and their captions:

```
captions-1a.css (excerpt)
.captioned_photo {
  float: right;
  margin: .5em 0 .5em 2em;
  padding: 0;
  line-height: 1em;
  width: 240px;
}
.captioned_photo p {
  width: 100%;
  margin: 0;
  padding: 1em 0;
  font: .75em/1.75em Verdana, sans-serif;
  color: #666;
}
.captioned_photo img {
  margin: 0;
  padding: 0;
  display: block;
}
```

This CSS floats the containing **div**, which has a class of **captioned_photo** that holds the image and the caption, so that the page's body text will wrap around both, as in Figure 2.21.

Figure 2.21: The styled caption appearing below the image

Another, slightly different way to lay out the page would be to place the caption to the side of the image. This is what the CSS would look like:

captions-1b.css (excerpt)

```
.captioned_photo {
  float: right;
  margin: .5em -2em 2em 2em;
  padding: 0;
  line-height: 1em;
  width: 360px;
}
.captioned_photo p {
  width: 25%;
  margin: 80px 0 0 2em;
  padding: 1em 0;
  font: .75em/1.75em Verdana, sans-serif;
  color: #666;
  float: left;
}
.captioned_photo img {
  margin: 0;
  padding: 0;
  display: block;
  float: left;
}
```

The result of this markup appears in Figure 2.22.

Figure 2.22: The styled caption appearing beside the image

These methods usually serve their purposes well. However, if you're a designer, you probably want *your* page to look a little more interesting, right? Of course you do!

My favorite way to display captions is to position them on top of the image. Let's look at the different ways in which this can be done.

Experimenting with Stacking and Transparencies

The basic page markup will be the same for the all of these captioning examples, the only difference is that you could change the **_src_** attreibute of **_img_** to images/captions-2.jpg. These next two cases experiment with alpha transparencies, the use of which I encourage, especially now that Internet Explorer 7 has transparent PNG support.

Take a look at Figure 2.23, which shows a semi-transparent caption overlaid on an image.

Figure 2.23: A semi-transparent caption

> ### NOTE   *Alpha Transparency in Internet Explorer 6 and Earlier*
>
> Alpha Transparency works well in most browsers; unfortunately, to have it work in Internet Explorer versions 5, 5.5, and 6, we need to add an additional style and set a **filter** property, which is proprietary to Internet Explorer. We can use conditional comments (also a proprietary IE feature) to serve up additional styles to Internet Explorer versions earlier than 7:
>
> ```
> <!--[if lt IE 7]>
> <style type="text/css">
> .captioned_photo p {
>   background: none;
>   filter:progid:DXImageTransform.Microsoft.AlphaImageLoader
>       (sizingMethod=scale, src='images/caption-white.png');
> }
> </style>
> <![endif]-->
> ```
>
> The **filter** used in this CSS example can't be paired with a **background**, as that background will be used instead, without alpha transparency. You can put this rule in a separate, external style sheet, instead of embedding the styles, if you so choose, though adding another HTTP request for such a small addition is likely to slow down your site.
>
> More information on PNG transparencies is available in Michael Lovitt's article "Cross-Browser Variable Opacity with PNG: A Real Solution,"[1] and at Microsoft's AlphaImageLoader Filter page.[2]

The caption is positioned at the bottom of the image, and is able to expand to fit the amount of content placed within it. However, I recommend that the caption remains only a couple of lines long at most—if it's any longer, it will cover too much of the image.

1   http://alistapart.com/stories/pngopacity/
2   http://alistapart.com/stories/pngopacity/

The caption is translucent, because it uses a transparent background image. To create the background image needed for this example, we create a 1x1px graphic consisting of a single layer filled with white at 75% opacity. We save this graphic as a PNG-24 with transparency turned on.

Adding Style

As I mentioned, the basic page styles will remain the same for each of these examples—we'll just change the CSS for the captioned photo. Here are the changes you'll need to make to create the caption shown in Figure 2.24:

captions-2a.css (excerpt)

```css
.captioned_photo {
  position: relative;
  float: right;
  margin: .5em 0 .5em 1.25em;
  padding: 0;
  border: 3px double #4d4d4d;
  line-height: 1em;
}
.captioned_photo p {
  position: absolute;
  bottom: 0;
  left: 0;
  width: 100%;
  margin: 0;
  padding: 0;
  background: url(images/caption-white.png);
  font: .75em/1.25em Verdana, sans-serif;
  letter-spacing:.05em;
  color: #000;
}
.captioned_photo p span {
  display: block;
  padding: .75em;
}
.captioned_photo img {
  margin: 0;
  padding: 0;
  display: block;
}
```

Let's walk through this CSS together. We need to set the containing **div** with a **class** of **captioned_photo** to use relative positioning, since we're positioning the caption on top of the image. We choose to **float** the image to the right. The image will be set so that the margins line up with the text at its top and to its right, and so that some additional spacing is applied on the caption's bottom and right. The margin sizes for your floated image container will vary in accordance with the direction in which you want your image to float, and how you've set your paragraph margins, padding, and letter spacing.

In this example, we want to have a 3px border on the containing `div`. We also need to set the line height to `1em` to make sure that the caption text stays tight. The caption is placed in a paragraph, so the `width` set for `p.captioned_photo` should be set to `100%` so that it will fill the entire `width` of the image. We can use a `span` to set the `padding` so that the use of hacks won't be necessary. Applying a span also gives us room for extra styling we may desire. The caption fonts are relative to those set in the `body`, so you may want to adjust these to suit your tastes.

So much can be done with styling image captions. Experiment!

Adding More Style

The example in Figure 2.24 uses two background images, one of which is translucent. To create the caption background image needed for this example, we'll create a 200×1px graphic consisting of a black, horizontal gradient at 50% opacity, which allows more of the photo to show through than would be possible with a solid background image. Darker images are recommended for this example, since white text is used for the caption.

Figure 2.24: A variation on the semi-transparent caption

The CSS that creates the display shown in Figure 2.24 is as follows:

captions-2b.css (excerpt)

```
.captioned_photo {
  position: relative;
  float: left;
  display: block;
  margin: .5em 1.25em .5em 0;
  padding: 1em;
  border: 1px solid #ccc;
  border-top-color: #eee;
  border-right-color: #ddd;
  border-bottom-color: #bbb;
  background: url(images/bg.gif) bottom left repeat-x;
  line-height: 1em;
}
```

```
.captioned_photo p {
  position: absolute;
  bottom: 2.25em;
  left: 1.375em;
  display: block;
  width: 240px; /* Needs to match the width of the image */
  margin: 0;
  padding: 0;
  background: url(images/caption-black.png) top left repeat-y;
  font: .75em/1.25em Verdana, sans-serif;
  letter-spacing:.05em;
  color: #fff;
}
.captioned_photo p span {
  display: block;
  padding: 1em;
}
.captioned_photo img {
  margin: 0 0 -.0625em 0;
  padding: 0;
}
```

A lot of these styles are very similar to those we've used in previous examples. However, in this version, we're floating the image to the left, so we switch what was previously a left-side margin to the right. We've also added **padding** of **1em** to the **captioned_photo** declaration and changed the **border** to have a **width** value of **1px**.

We want a slightly three-dimensional look, but since the **outset border-style** can be unpredictable, I recommend choosing similar colors to help give a feeling of light, as we saw earlier in Figure 2.4. We also applied the background image shown in Figure 2.25 to the bottom of the containing **div** and repeated it along the X axis. The image is a subtle light gray gradient that moves from light gray at the bottom to white at the top.

Figure 2.25: Gradient background

As we've changed the **padding**, we need to reposition the caption a little. We can move it up above the bottom of the image, to make the display a little more interesting.

The paragraph's **width** needs to change to reflect the size of the image, or the caption will bleed off the edge on the right as a result of the **padding** that we added to this element earlier. We only want the background image to repeat along the X axis, starting from the bottom left, since a repeating pattern wouldn't look good with this gradient.

Finally, the image's `margin` is adjusted to make sure that it fits within the "frame" created by the surrounding `div`. Once again, to make the display work in Internet Explorer 6 and earlier, you'll need to add the transparency filter that was explained in the note called "Alpha Transparency in Internet Explorer 6 and Earlier" on page 59.

Creating an Offset Caption

For the next example, shown in Figure 2.26, it is important that we avoid relying on additional imagery. We still want the caption to sit on top of the image, but we want to offset it slightly from the image, to give it a unique look. This is my favorite example—it's a little different from what I'm used to seeing on web sites. So that your design matches the example, change the `src` attribute of your `img` element to **"images/captions-3.jpg"**.

Adding Style

Here's the CSS we'll use for this example:

captions-3.css (excerpt)

```
.captioned_photo {
  position: relative;
  float: right;
  display: block;
  margin: .5em 0 .5em 1.25em;
  padding: 0;
  border: 3px solid #333;
  line-height: 1em;
}
.captioned_photo p {
  position: absolute;
  bottom: 14px;
  left: 0;
  display: block;
  width: 240px; /* Needs to match the width of the image */
  margin: 0 0 0 1.5em;
  padding: 0;
  border: 1px solid #666;
  border-right-color: #000;
  border-bottom-color: #000;
  background-color: #111;
  font: .75em/1.25em Verdana, sans-serif;
  letter-spacing:.05em;
  color: #fff;
}
```

```
.captioned_photo p span {
  display: block;
  padding: .75em;
}
.captioned_photo img {
  margin: 0;
  padding: 0;
  display: block;
  border: 1px solid #fff;
}
```

This example is similar to the last, except that the caption floats to the right. The `border` for `captioned_photo` is set to 3px. The caption also uses a `padding` of `1em`, so, again, we need to set the paragraph's `width` to the size of the image. The bottom positioning and left `margin` of the paragraph are adjusted so that the caption is located the same distance from the left and bottom edges of the image. That image, which now has a `margin` set to `0`, can have a `border` as well, so we give it a single-pixel white border. The result, Figure 2.26, is really quite effective.

Figure 2.26: An offset caption

That's all for our experimentation in this chapter, but a whole world of great examples of images at work in CSS is available online. Let's explore just a few of these resources next.

Further Resources

The Internet offers countless examples of photo galleries and contextual image styles that have been created by very talented designers and developers. This is a shortlist of my favorites, which I recommend as being great examples of well-designed galleries:

- **Experiments with wide images, by Richard Rutter,** at http://clagnut.com/sandbox/imagetest/
- **CSS: figures & captions, by Bert Bos,** at http://w3.org/Style/Examples/007/figures.html
- **Floating an image and caption, by Russ Weakley,** at http://css.maxdesign.com.au/floatutorial/tutorial0211.htm

- **Hoverbox Image Gallery, by Nathan Smith,** at http://host.sonspring.com/hoverbox/
- **Photos, by Douglas Bowman,** at http://dbowman.com/photos/
- **CSS Play | Demos – Photo galleries, by Stu Nicholls,** at http://cssplay.co.uk/menu/
- **Drop Shadow Gallery, by Brian Williams,** at http://alistapart.com/d/onionskin/gallery.html
- **Lightbox JS v2.0, by Lokesh Dhakar,** at http://huddletogether.com/projects/lightbox2/

With the pages you've worked on throughout this chapter, and the above links, you have plenty of examples to refer to!

Summary

Now that you have some examples to follow, I encourage you to experiment and find interesting ways to display your images!

In this chapter, we've seen how we can use the deceptively simple concepts of space and color to create a level of visual impact that's similar to that achieved by real-life art galleries. We've worked through a number of different examples, and explored the markup that achieves each effect. We've learned a lot about the presentation of contextual images—in both introductory and captioned forms—and discussed many different techniques that you can use to set your web site's images apart from the rest.

A design instructor once taught me that design is not about what you can add to a composition, but what you can take away while retaining a strong design. The underlying theme of this chapter has been that while it's great to add some visual interest to your images, it's vital to remember that the styles you choose should provide an elegant accent to your images—not a distraction.

Backgrounds

Deadwood design is Australia's 47th best
web design and development agency.

We specialise in awesomeness.

For many years, web sites all over the world generously offered free tiled background patterns to budding young web designers as a way of "enhancing" their web pages. Derided by many designers in the field as tacky, these backgrounds were generally used sparingly, if at all, by professional designers, especially where download speed was of major concern—and in those heady days of 14.4kbps modems, download speed was *always* of major concern.

How times have changed in the past ten or so years! With the advent of CSS and the increased proliferation of broadband, backgrounds have become an integral part of web design and development. Backgrounds are no longer simple repeated patterns or, in more abstract cases, extremely large photographs. Nowadays, they form the basis of many a well-designed site. From CSS rollovers and "Faux Column" layouts, to form styling and fluid layouts, backgrounds have become an integral part of the developer's toolkit.

In this chapter, we'll first of all deal with the theory behind the, um, background, in which we'll break down the properties of backgrounds. Armed with this theory, we'll proceed to walk through a case study together, in order to see some of the techniques that are utilized by developers faced with a challenging and daunting site design. Finally, we'll predict the advent of CSS 3, speculating as to what may be in store for designers in the near future.

Background Basics

Before we begin our case study, we'll need to be equipped with an understanding of the basics of creating backgrounds. For the sake of keeping this instruction brief and concise, let's just look at the shorthand notation of the **background** property to start with. It looks like this:

```
body {
  background: #1299AB url(images/myBackground.gif) no-repeat
     fixed 10% 50px;
}
```

That's your background, right there. But to the uninitiated, this code probably doesn't make a whole lot of sense. Let's break it down into its individual properties—**background-color**, **background-image**, **background-repeat**, **background-attachment**, and **background-position**.

Setting **background-color**

Let's take a look at the specification of the **background-color** property:

```
body {
  background: #1299AB url(images/myBackground.gif) no-repeat
     fixed 10% 50px;
}
```

This property can take as its value a hexadecimal number, an RGB color name value, for example, **rgb(255,0,0)** for red, a name value, or a transparent keyword.

Hexadecimal values use the fewest characters, and are the most common method of defining colors in CSS. So, for simplicity, we'll use hexadecimal values.[3]

Setting **background-image**

The **background-image** property is also very straightforward:

```
body {
  background: #1299AB url(images/myBackground.gif) no-repeat
     fixed 10% 50px;
}
```

This property gives us most of our design flexibility. The location of the image should be specified relative to your CSS file. For example, if you keep your images in a subdirectory

---

3   A detailed list of valid color name values can be found at http://www.w3schools.com/css/css_colornames.asp.

of the folder containing your CSS files, and this subdirectory is called *images*, you'd need to edit the location of the image like so:

```
body {
  background: #1299AB url(images/myBackground.gif) no-repeat
    fixed 10% 50px;
}
```

Simple!

Setting `background-repeat`

Here's the **background-repeat** property:

```
body {
  background: #1299AB url(images/myBackground.gif) no-repeat
    fixed 10% 50px;
}
```

The valid values for the `background-repeat` property are:

- **no-repeat**

  As its name suggests, the `no-repeat` value causes the `background-image` to be rendered once, at the point determined by the `background-position` property.

- **repeat-x**

  `repeat-x` forces the background image to repeat horizontally, left-to-right.

- **repeat-y**

  Setting `background-repeat` to `repeat-y` results in the image being repeated along the Y axis, starting at the top of the element.

- **repeat**

  The default value for `background-repeat`, `repeat` causes the `background-image` to be tiled across the entire area of the element, starting from the top left.

Setting `background-attachment`

Let's investigate the `background-attachment` property:

```
body {
  background: #1299AB url(images/myBackground.gif) no-repeat
    fixed 10% 50px;
}
```

The only valid values for this property are:

- **fixed**
- **scroll**, the default value

The `background-attachment` property defines whether the `background-position` is calculated relative to the page content (`scroll`), or relative to the browser viewport (`fixed`). The most notable difference between these values is that `background-attachment: fixed;` will cause the `background-image` to remain stationary if the user scrolls the page.

For the purposes of this chapter, we'll ignore the `background-attachment` property, and it'll therefore assume the default value. We'll gloss over the `background-attachment` property, due to the lack of support for the `fixed` value in Internet Explorer 6, which still holds a large share of the browser market despite the release of IE 7. IE 6 only supports `background-attachment: fixed;` on the `body` element.

Setting `background-position`

Here's the `background-position` property:

```
body {
  background: #1299AB url(images/myBackground.gif) no-repeat
      fixed 10% 50px;
}
```

The `background-position` property defines the starting X and Y coordinates of the background image. Keywords (`left`/`right`/`center`/`top`/`bottom`), relative (percentage) values, or absolute values (`px`/`em`/`pt`/`mm`) are valid options for setting the `background-position`.

The horizontal keywords that determine the X position of the background image are:

- **left**, the default
- **center**
- **right**

The vertical keywords which determine the Y position are:

- **top**, the default
- **center**
- **bottom**

Case Study: Deadwood Design

That was a very quick tour, but you now have all you need to create stunning and functional backgrounds. So, let's get into the fun stuff!

Let's imagine that it's 8.30 on a Monday morning, and you've just walked into your office to find the mockup in Figure 3.1 in your inbox, with love from your inhouse designer. What we have here is a fictitious company called Deadwood Design, whose web site we have to build.

Figure 3.1: The design mockup

You're still a little groggy from your big weekend, and at first glance it all seems fairly straightforward. But let's look more closely at all the elements that make up this design. Gradients? Check. Patterns? Check. Images? Check. But, just a second …

The designer has requested that the design be made **fluid**, or **liquid**, meaning that it should be able to adapt in height and width to the user's browser, while retaining the desired proportions. Every feature situated to the left of the tree in Figure 3.1 must therefore remain in its existing position, no matter what. The tree and the logo, however, must have the ability to move further to the right as users increase the size of their browsers. That said, the tree must remain anchored to the bottom of the layout at all times.

"Dude … what?" you think to yourself.

Never fear, Grasshopper, we're here to help. To succeed in our chosen field of endeavor, we must first start at the bottom—which is exactly what we're going to do now. We need to get rid of those pesky elements on the page, and take a look at how we need to construct the background image for the **body** element. This job poses quite the challenge, but we're up for it! The first decision we need to make is where to begin our work. The answer, of course, is with the background.

Take a look at Figure 3.2. As you can see, it's an average run-of-the-mill gradient that we can create right now in Photoshop, Fireworks, GIMP, or any graphics application of your choice. If you look closely, you'll find that the gradation actually ends about three-quarters of the way down the page, and the lighter gray makes up the rest of the page.

Figure 3.2: The bare-bones background

Let's crop this image to a height of 550px, to produce the background in Figure 3.3.

Figure 3.3: The cropped gradient

This image doesn't change at any point along its X axis: the only color changes occur on the Y axis. What this means is that, rather than trying to use this large image as our background, we can cut a slice of it, from top to bottom, and repeat that tall, skinny image across the page. As I'm sure you've guessed, this supports our goal of being able to increase the width of the page automatically, in response to the resizing of user's browser.

Now we can start our CSS file! Here's the **body** declaration we'll need:

```
body {
  background: #A4A4A4 url(images/bg_gradient.png) repeat-x;
}
```

As you can see, we've set the **background-color** of the body to gray (**#A4A4A4**), and repeated the gradient image along the X axis only.

Figure 3.4: The tree image

Now we'll create the tree image in Figure 3.4, and anchor that to the lower-right corner of the browser viewport. The best way to create this image is either to save it as a transparent PNG, or create a GIF by placing the tree on top of a gray background (**#A4A4A4**) and knocking out that gray when you export the file.

At this point, the body of our HTML document is empty, so let's begin to flesh it out by adding a **div** with an **id** of **tree**—this empty element will be used as the styling hook we need to add the transparent tree image:

```
<body>
  <div id="tree"></div>
</body>
```

Our next task is to style this **div**. First, we add the background image, but, this time, we don't want the tree to repeat on either the X or Y axis:

```
#tree {
  background: url(images/tree.gif) no-repeat;
}
```

You'll notice that we've skipped setting a **background-color** here. The default value of **background-color** is **transparent**, which happens to be exactly the property we're after—no color setting is required!

Now we need to anchor the tree **div** to the lower-right corner of the browser, so we'll have to position it absolutely. We'll set it flush against the bottom, and 40px from the right-hand side of the page:

```
#tree {
  background: url(images/tree.gif) no-repeat;
  position: absolute;
  bottom: 0;
  right: 40px;
}
```

And we'd better not forget to specify a **width** and **height** equal to the dimensions of the tree image:

```
#tree {
  background: url(images/tree.gif) no-repeat;
  position: absolute;
  bottom: 0;
  right: 40px;
  width: 331px;
  height: 400px;
}
```

Let's load that page into a browser—we should see something similar to Figure 3.5.

Figure 3.5: Previewing the page in a browser

Now it's time to insert our trusty corporate logo. We'll need to follow much the same process for this image as we did for the tree, ensuring that the **background** is still transparent.

We need to add an **h1** with an **id** of **logo** to the HTML to provide a meaningful title for the page. The text will be replaced using the **text-indent** method covered in Chapter 1:

```
<body>
  <h1 id="logo">Deadwood Design</h1>
  <div id="tree"></div>
</body>
```

We want to position the logo 40px in from the right, just like the tree, but this time we need to position it relatively from the top of the document. Positioning the image relatively (using a percentage value) from the top means that the web site will fit reasonably well onto screens set at lower resolutions, as a reduction in the height of the browser will lessen the distance between the top of the viewport and the logo. We'll also use the **text-indent** property to negatively position the **h1** text off the page:

```
#logo {
  background: url(images/logo.gif) no-repeat;
  position: absolute;
  top: 15%;
  right: 40px;
  width: 334px;
  height: 36px;
  text-indent: -9999em;
  margin: 0;
}
```

Now let's see what we have; your display should reflect Figure 3.6.

Figure 3.6: Previewing the positioned logo

If we resize the browser to an 800×600px resolution, as shown in Figure 3.7, we notice that the tree appears to be overwritten by the logo, which doesn't detract from the design too much. It actually looks quite nice, no?

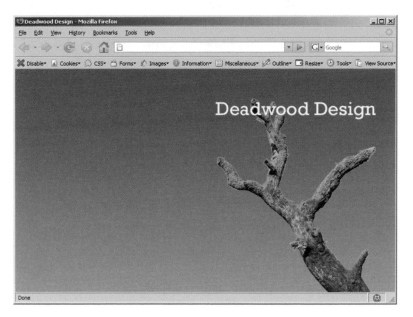

Figure 3.7: Previewing the logo and tree image at an 800×600px resolution

The next task is to create the introductory paragraph. In the mockup we saw in Figure 3.1, the first D in the paragraph was an image, while the rest of the text appeared to be good ol' standard HTML text.

We'll export the D accompanied by green squares as a transparent GIF, and assign it as the **background-image** of a **div** with an **id** of **intro**, which should turn out like Figure 3.8:

```
<body>
  <h1 id="logo">Deadwood Design</h1>
  <div id="intro">
    <p>Deadwood design is Australia's 47th best web design and
       development agency.</p>
    <p>We specialise in awesomeness.</p>
  </div>
  <div id="tree"></div>
</body>
```

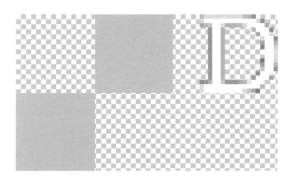

Figure 3.8: The D

Even though the first letter of the sentence—D—is an image, we still need to include that D in the HTML so that search engines, screen readers, and CSS-incapable browsers can still make sense of the text. After all, "eadwood design" won't help anybody, will it?

Let's insert the D into a **span**, and position that **span** off the page so it's still available to assistive devices:

```
<body>
  <h1 id="logo">Deadwood Design</h1>
  <div id="intro">
    <p><span>D</span>eadwood design is Australia's 47th best
        web design and development agency.</p>
    <p>We specialise in awesomeness.</p>
  </div>
  <div id="tree"></div>
</body>
```

Next, we'll position the **intro div** 15% from the top and 40px from the left of the boundaries of the **body** element. To ensure the text doesn't run over the top of the **intro div**'s **background-image**, we'll put 61px of padding on the image's left-hand side, and 5px on its top, to create the display shown in Figure 3.8:

```
#intro {
  position: absolute;
  top: 15%;
  left: 40px;
  background: url(images/d.gif) no-repeat;
  padding: 5px 0 0 61px;
  width: 250px;
}
#intro span {
  position: absolute;
  top: -1000px;
}
#intro p {
  margin: 0 0 12px 0;
  color: #fff;
  font-family: Georgia, sans-serif;
  font-size: 0.8em;
}
```

Figure 3.8: The introductory paragraph

Now it's on to the portfolio section of the page, which is to be a series of six links to different pages showcasing Deadwood Design's portfolio. This is where the job becomes a bit tricky—the page mockup includes a checkered pattern that extends across the entire page and sits underneath the tree image. The easiest way to achieve this effect is to place the portfolio **div** above the tree **div** in the page markup:

```
<body>
  <h1 id="logo">Deadwood Design</h1>
  <div id="intro">
    <p><span>D</span>eadwood design is Australia's 47th best
      web design and development agency.</p>
    <p>We specialise in awesomeness.</p>
  </div>
  <div id="portfolio"></div>
  <div id="tree"></div>
</body>
```

Theoretically, we could put an unordered list inside the portfolio **div** and assign the light checkered pattern as the background to the **div**. Unfortunately, our old friend Internet Explorer lays waste to our plans with its incorrect implementation of the **z-index** property. Because of this, we have to put the **ul** outside of the **div**, as shown in the following code:

```
<body>
  <h1 id="logo">Deadwood Design</h1>
  <div id="intro">
    <p><span>D</span>eadwood design is Australia's 47th best
       web design and development agency.</p>
    <p>We specialise in awesomeness.</p>
  </div>
<ul>
   <li><a href="1.html"><img src="images/portfolio1.jpg"
      alt="Mountains and Sky"/></a></li>
   <li><a href="2.html"><img src="images/portfolio2.jpg"
      alt="Lampshade"/></a></li>
   <li><a href="3.html"><img src="images/portfolio3.jpg"
      alt="Cat"/></a></li>
   <li><a href="4.html"><img src="images/portfolio4.jpg"
      alt="Bark"/></a></li>
   <li><a href="5.html"><img src="images/portfolio5.jpg"
      alt="Thumbs Up"/></a></li>
   <li><a href="6.html"><img src="images/portfolio6.jpg"
      alt="Flowers"/></a></li>
</ul>
<div id="portfolio"></div>  <div id="tree"></div>
</body>
```

We'll position the portfolio **div** and the **ul** 35% of the way down the page, and assign the checkered background GIF shown in Figure 3.9 as the **background-image** of the **div**.

Figure 3.9: A 4px square background pattern—checkered areas indicate transparent pixels

Having said that, repeating tiny GIF files can cause browsers on less-capable computers to work quite slowly. It's a good idea to create a slightly bigger image, so let's do that now:

```
#portfolio {
  position: absolute;
  top: 35%;
  left: 0;
  width: 100%;
  height: 294px;
  background: url(images/bg_checkered.gif);
}
```

Figure 3.10 depicts the 40px-square image we'll be using as the checkered background.

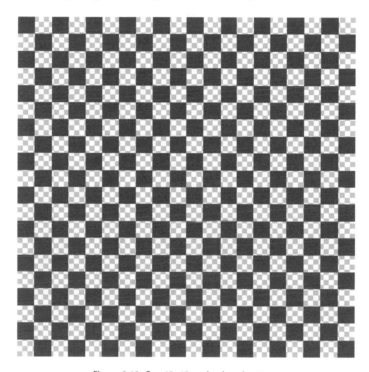

Figure 3.10: Our 40x40px checkered pattern

We also need to style the unordered list, and its list items. We've created another checkered image similar to the one used for the background of our portfolio **div**; the only difference is that this image's dimensions are 8x8px, and it is slightly darker than the one that repeats across the page:

```
#portfolio ul {
  list-style: none inside;
  width: 482px;
  margin: 0;
}
```

```
#portfolio ul li {
  width: 138px;
  height: 138px;
  float: left;
  margin: 0 18px 18px 0;
  background: url(images/bg_checkered_dark.gif);
}
#portfolio ul li a {
  float: left;
  width: 102px;
  height: 102px;
  margin: 18px 0 0 18px;
}

#portfolio ul li a img {
  border: 0;
}
```

Have a look at Figure 3.11—it's all starting to come together!

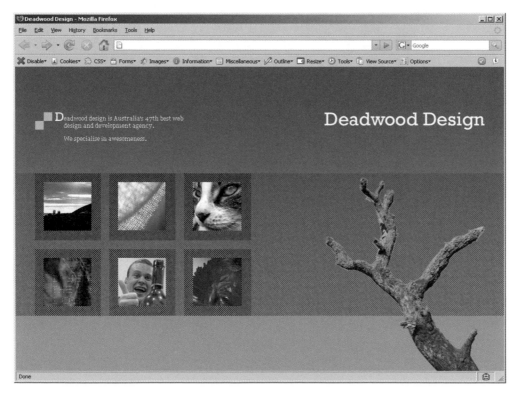

Figure 3.11: Design following the addition of thumbnails

However, if we resize the browser window to 800×600px, as shown in Figure 3.12, we see what's commonly referred to as a "whoopsie."

Figure 3.12: Whoopsie! The design breaks at 800×600px

As you can see, my housemate's cat, Miette, now has a branch through her eye (she'd be *so* unimpressed) and our finely crafted logo is obstructed by the top of the tree. Not only that, but we can't click on the last two thumbnails because the tree image is obstructing them. Oh dear, this is clearly unacceptable!

Let's remain calm, though. We can easily evade this problem by defining a **z-index** for the logo and the unordered list containing our portfolio images. Positioned elements (those that have **position: absolute;**, **position: relative;**, or **position: fixed;**) have an automatically assigned stack order, or **z-index**, that defines how any overlaps should be handled—elements with a higher **z-index** will overlap those with a lower **z-index**. To gain the ability to set the **z-index** of the unordered list explicitly, we'll set its **position** to **relative**, which will have no effect on the physical position of the list within our design:

```
#logo {
  position: absolute;
  top: 15%;
  right: 40px;
  width: 334px;
  height: 36px;
  background: url(images/logo.gif) no-repeat;
  text-indent: -9999em;
  margin: 0;
  z-index: 3;
}
```

```
...
#portfolio ul {
  position: relative;
  z-index: 4;
  list-style: none inside;
  width: 482px;
  margin: 0;
}
```

We can see that in Figure 3.13, the tree image is sitting *below* the thumbnails, and the hyperlinks are still accessible.

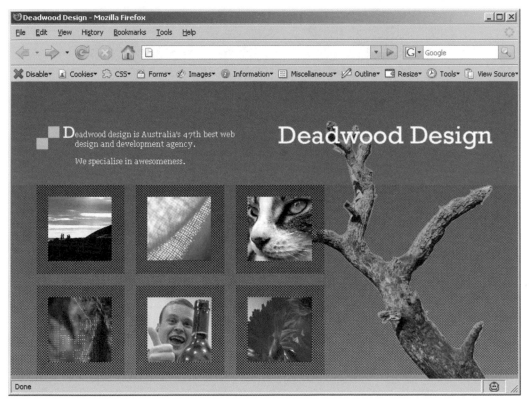

Figure 3.13: Checking the page again—**z-index** to the rescue!

There we have it! Figure 3.14 shows our completely fluid page, which looks good at any resolution, and was completed in fewer than 80 lines of CSS! Not as daunting as you thought, was it?

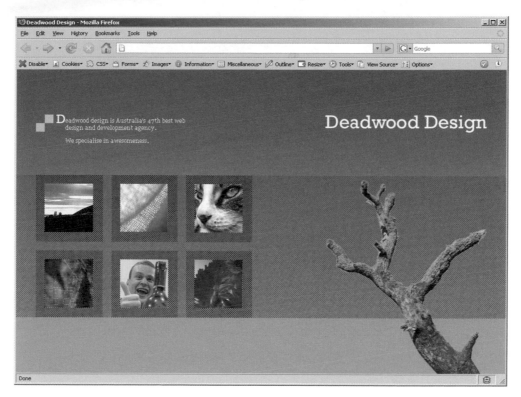

Figure 3.14: Viewing the completed page at 1024x768px

The Future of Backgrounds

With CSS 3 currently under construction and coming our way, it's a great time to discuss the future of CSS design in relation to backgrounds. Let's have a quick look at the nifty changes that have been proposed, as well as those that have been implemented already and are available on certain platforms.

The Possibility of Multiple Backgrounds

That's right, no more **tag soup**—documents that forego semantic markup in favour of presentation. We might go out of our way to avoid tag soup right now, but CSS 3 will allow for the attachment of multiple background images to a single element, like this:

```
#mydiv {
  background:url('top.gif') top left repeat-x, url('right.gif')
    top right repeat-y, url('bottom.gif') bottom left repeat-x,
    url('left.gif') top left repeat-y;
}
```

With CSS 3, results such as those shown in Figure 3.15 will be very easy to achieve using a single **div** element. How cool is that?

Figure 3.15: Multiple background images applied to one element

At the time of writing, only the WebKit rendering engine and Safari 1.3 and later support multiple backgrounds.

Looking at `background-size`

One really nice CSS feature is **background-size**, which allows us to assign an absolute or relative size to a background image. In theory, no matter what size a client's browser is, the background image would always fit perfectly onto the screen, and no part of the image would be cut off. (Whether it looks good or not is another matter entirely!)

At the time of writing, only Safari and Konqueror support this feature.

Defining `background-origin`

The starting point for the calculation of the **background-position** property of an element is determined by **background-origin**. We can apply any of three values to this property:

- **border**
- **padding**
- **content**

If we apply the **border** value, the calculations for the background image's position will start from the edge of the border of the element. If you select the **padding** value, the **background-image** starts from the far edge of the padding. If you use the **content** value, the **background-**

`image` starts from the edge of the first child element. The differences between these three values are illustrated in Figure 3.16.

Figure 3.16: The three different values of **background-origin**, and their effects

At the time of writing, only Mozilla, Safari, and Konqueror supported `background-origin`.

Summary

As we've seen in this chapter, the humble and retiring background has really come a long way in the past ten or so years. No longer having to be either invisible or garish, the background can now add enormously to supporting the designer's vision. Nowadays, backgrounds are a fundamental aspect of not only proving a designer's vision, but enabling them to push the aesthetic envelope.

This chapter has provided an overview of the CSS properties of the background, and our case study of the page layout for Deadwood Design has demonstrated these properties in action. We gained a solid understanding of the behavior of the **background** property as we used it for this practical application, and in so doing, have learned ways of avoiding various background problems.

We've looked towards the future of CSS, which promises that we'll be able to implement intricate and detailed designs while keeping our code as simple as possible. Now we just have to wait in the hope that browser vendors implement it consistently, so we can all start to live a hack-free lifestyle!

Navigation

The art of navigation dates back over 6,000 years. Vast civilizations thrived due to the skill, mathematics, and keen intuition of their navigators. Imagine making a voyage across the Atlantic Ocean with no real sense of direction! To your visitors, your web site is like that ocean. As the cartographer—read developer—it's your job to provide your visitors with simple, obvious directions to their destinations. Although, in this instance, poor navigation may not be a matter of life and death, it may mean the difference between a successful visit or a frustrating experience for your web site's users.

In this chapter, we'll work together through a project for a fictional client—let's call it Cartography Corner. We're the lucky people who get to work on the project behind the scenes, while a front-end designer liaises with the client. Let's imagine that this particular client is a demanding one, who won't be happy until we've exhausted all options for presenting his navigation system. It suits our purposes for this chapter, and after all, in the real world, some clients really do seem sent to try us!

First, let's walk through the basic markup that's essential to developing any navigation system. Then we'll meet each of the major navigation types in turn, looking closely at the intricacies of vertical, horizontal, and tabbed navigation systems in all their glorious detail.

background-position: 0 0;

Home

und-position: -127px 0;

Home

Home

Home

Maps

Journal

History

References

Contact

Safari

References

Contact

Firefox

References

Contact

Internet Explorer 6

The Markup

Successful navigation starts with the proper markup. Taking current convention and proper semantics as our guide, we'll mark up our navigational links using an unordered list. This'll form the beginning of our client's navigation system:

```
<ul>
  <li><a href="/">Home</a></li>
  <li><a href="/maps/">Maps</a></li>
  <li><a href="/journal/">Journal</a></li>
  <li><a href="/history/">History</a></li>
  <li><a href="/references/">References</a></li>
  <li><a href="/contact/">Contact</a></li>
</ul>
```

The basic elements are all there: the navigation items are in a list, and the links are in place. But how are we to distinguish this list from any other unordered list on the page? There should only be one navigation list per page, so a common solution is to place this list inside a **div** with an **id** of **nav**. This method will work just fine, but unless you need another block-level element for styling purposes, I suggest that you simply put that **id** directly on the list itself. Unordered lists are also block-level elements, just like **div** elements—something we'll take advantage of when we style the navigation using CSS.

Similarly, we often need to be able to isolate one specific navigation item from its companions when managing the presentation. This is easily achieved—we simply place a unique **id** attribute on each item in the unordered list. Let's see what our markup looks like now:

vertical.html (excerpt)

```
<ul id="nav">
  <li id="nav_hom"><a href="/">Home</a></li>
  <li id="nav_map"><a href="/maps/">Maps</a></li>
  <li id="nav_jou"><a href="/journal/">Journal</a></li>
  <li id="nav_his"><a href="/history/">History</a></li>
  <li id="nav_ref"><a href="/references/">References</a></li>
  <li id="nav_con"><a href="/contact/">Contact</a></li>
</ul>
```

Fantastic! We've created the foundation code from which we can develop any of the currently accepted types of navigation menu. Putting this code in place wasn't too difficult, and the following sections, in which we'll style these foundations to appear vertically, horizontally, and in tabbed format, won't be much harder.

Basic Vertical Navigation

Now that we've established our markup, we can begin coding our styles. To start with, we'll style our navigation list to look like the mockup shown in Figure 4.1.

Figure 4.1: Designer's navigation mockup

This mockup came from the front-end designer we're working with on the Cartography Corner project, and looking at it, we notice a couple of terrific features right from the beginning. First, the hover state of the links shows a slightly darker background. Second, the clickable area seems to extend the whole width of the navigation area and height of the list item—a big plus for the interface's usability. We'd better remember to give the designer a pat on the back for considering our users!

> **NOTE   A Word on Accessibility**
>
> It's important to make sure that your navigation is obviously and accessibly styled to meet the needs of the specific audience that'll use your site. When you're designing and styling a site, be sure to stay user-centric to maximize that site's overall usability. As you just saw, for instance, it's helpful to make the clickable area as large as possible when styling any link. There's more information on this topic available online.[4]

Styling the Unordered List

Working from the outside in, let's start with an example of a page font specification involving the `html` and `body` elements, then style our unordered list element. As the font for the navigation will most likely match that of the rest of the page, the `font-family` should be declared much higher in the cascade:

vertical.css (excerpt)

```
html {
  font: small/1.4 "Lucida Grande", Tahoma, sans-serif;
}
body {
  font-size: 92%;
}
```

4   http://www.sitepoint.com/subcat/accessibility/

```
#nav {
  margin: 0;
  padding: 0;
  background: #6F6146;
  list-style-type: none;
  width: 180px;
}
```

If we view our work in a browser, we'll see something like Figure 4.2.

Figure 4.2: Our progress so far

Now we need to decide which element we need to style to implement the design mockup. It would be easy for us to apply the white border and padding on the list item, and style the text color and text decoration on the anchor. But that approach wouldn't give us the large clickable area that's shown in the mockup. In order to make each link into a larger, clickable block, we need to apply the padding to the anchor itself, and remove the default **margin** and **padding** from the list items.

Let's put those ideas into code:

vertical.css (excerpt)

```
#nav li {
  margin: 0;
  padding: 0;
}
#nav a {
  display: block;  /* to increase clickable area as a's default
      to inline */
  color: #FFF;
  text-decoration: none;
  padding: 0 15px;
  line-height: 2.5;  border-bottom:1px solid #FFF;
}
```

Styling the Last Menu Item

One subtle aspect that you might notice here is that the last navigation list item, **Contact**, will have a white bottom border. On a white background, that border won't be visible. However, it's a good idea to remove it, as the border will add a pixel to the height of your navigation. Since you won't see it, that invisible border may come back to haunt you if you run into positioning bugs down the road.

We specified **id** attributes for each list item element, so we can specifically target our last anchor to remove the unwanted border. Other than that, the only style rule we still need to add will apply to the **hover** pseudo-class; adding the rule will be easy now that we've given the anchor element the most real estate. Let's add those last two style rules now:

vertical.css (excerpt)

```
#nav #nav_con a {
  border: none;
}
#nav a:hover {
  background: #4F4532;
}
```

Let's make sure that our styles work as expected. Load up our navigation in Safari, Firefox, and Internet Explorer 6. Figure 4.3 shows what we see.

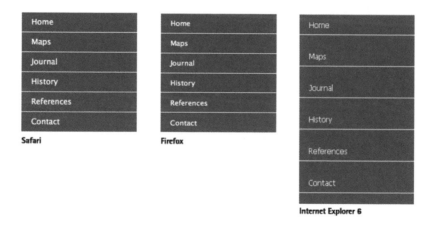

Figure 4.3: First browser check—IE's the odd one out

Oh no! Internet Explorer's gone all quirky. This bizarre treatment of list items is known as the "whitespace bug"—a phenomenon caused by IE's incorrect rendering of the whitespace between the list items.

Debugging for Internet Explorer

Fortunately, there's a quick workaround for the IE whitespace problem—we simply need to make some short additions to two of our element styles:

vertical.css (excerpt)

```
#nav {
  margin: 0;
  padding: 0;
  background: #6F6146;
  list-style-type: none;7
  width: 180px;
  float: left; /* Contain floated list items */
}
#nav li {
  margin: 0;
  padding: 0;
  float: left; /* This corrects the */
  width: 100%; /* IE whitespace bug */
}
```

By floating the list items, we trick IE into rendering them without any surrounding whitespace. However, to take this course of action requires us also to float the unordered list element in order to contain the floated list items, and extend our background color behind all of them. Because we've specified widths for both elements, the float property has no real side effects. At most, you may need to specify a **clear** property on an element below the navigation if you encounter any odd overlapping behavior. Be aware also that there are other ways to combat the IE whitespace bug, should floating fail to work for your particular page.[5]

NOTE Consistency Counts!

If you're using floats to style your navigation, stick with floats for the rest of your layout. If your layout requires the use of absolute positioning, it's easiest to style your navigation using absolute positioning. While there's nothing wrong with combining floats and positioning, it's much more confusing to try to debug code that uses both techniques. This note is by no means a rule, it's simply a recommendation.

Let's see how our browsers render the page with our new style properties applied; the results are shown in Figure 4.4.

Figure 4.4: Second, improved browser check

---

5   Roger Johanson of 456BereaStreet has a fine alternative in his article "Closing the gap between list items in IE," October 16, 2006, http://www.456bereastreet.com/archive/200610/closing_the_gap_between_list_items_in_ie/.

Excellent! Our navigation displays consistently, and hover states are working.

NOTE   Whitespace Woes

If you're still besieged by IE whitespace issues at this point, you can eradicate them by adjusting the markup slightly to remove the whitespace from between the list items. Here's an example:

```
<ul id="nav"
  ><li id="nav_hom"><a href="/">Home</a></li
  ><li id="nav_map"><a href="/maps/">Maps</a></li
  ><li id="nav_jou"><a href="/journal/">Journal</a></li
  ><li id="nav_his"><a href="/history/">History</a></li
  ><li id="nav_ref"><a href="/references/">References</a></li
  ><li id="nav_con"><a href="/contact/">Contact</a></li
></ul>
```

You'll observe that the last **>** is dropped from each open tag and placed directly before the **<** of the next open tag. This trick ensures that the markup for each navigation item remains indented and on its own line, but the whitespace between the elements is removed. In essence, whitespace between the elements has been removed. This way, the solution allows us to keep some semblance of formatting. Note, though, that this exercise will only work if you have *complete* control over the markup for the navigation.

But let's think again about what will happen when people actually use the site. It's helpful to indicate graphically within the navigation which area of the site the user is browsing. This type of display is often called **You Are Here** navigation, in reference to maps in public places that point out your current location. According to the designer of the Cartography Corner interface, the client wants us to create a You Are Here state for our navigation elements using a lighter colored background and dark brown, bold text for contrast. Let's set this style up.

Adding "You Are Here" Cues

One common way of indicating the navigation item that corresponds to the currently viewed page is by adding a **class** to the list item containing the anchor for that page. It looks like this:

```
<ul id="nav">
  <li id="nav_hom"><a href="/">Home</a></li>
  <li id="nav_map"><a href="/maps/">Maps</a></li>
  <li id="nav_jou"><a href="/journal/">Journal</a></li>
  <li id="nav_his"><a href="/history/">History</a></li>
  <li id="nav_ref" class="current"><a href="/references/">
    References</a></li>
  <li id="nav_con"><a href="/contact/">Contact</a></li>
</ul>
```

Here's the associated CSS:

```css
#nav li.current a {
  background: #BEB06F;
  color: #1A1303;
  font-weight: bold;
}
```

While this method can be effective, I like to take a more semantic approach. Considering that we may want to style multiple aspects of our pages—not just the navigation—differently for each section of the web site, it's a good idea to put an **id** attribute on the **body** element, to specify the page or section of the site the user is currently viewing:

vertical.html (excerpt)

```html
<body id="body_his">
  <ul id="nav">
    <li id="nav_hom"><a href="/">Home</a></li>
    <li id="nav_map"><a href="/maps/">Maps</a></li>
    <li id="nav_jou"><a href="/journal/">Journal</a></li>
    <li id="nav_his"><a href="/history/">History</a></li>
    <li id="nav_ref"><a href="/references/">References</a></li>
    <li id="nav_con"><a href="/contact/">Contact</a></li>
  </ul>
</body>
```

Now we simply need to specify the **id** property on the **body** for each section; then we can style the current navigational element:

vertical.css (excerpt)

```css
#body_hom #nav_hom a,
    #body_map #nav_map a,#body_jou #nav_jou a,
    #body_his #nav_his a,#body_ref #nav_ref a,
    #body_con #nav_con a {
  background: #BEB06F;
  color: #1A1303;
  font-weight: bold;
}
```

Sure, the style sheet gains a few more lines, but these additions mean that the navigation markup is always constant, and that can make life much easier for those maintaining the site. For example, we can now use a single include for the navigation on every page—we no longer have a need for multiple includes applied on a per-section basis, or for directly coding the navigation into each page.

Another benefit of this method is that our You Are Here navigation styles are much more specific than our normal hover-state styles. This means that the current navigation element for the currently viewed page or section will not change to reflect the hover styles when the user mouses over it, which makes it stand out even more.

Let's see our final navigation style sheet:

vertical.css (excerpt)

```
html {
  font: small/1.4 "Lucida Grande", Tahoma, sans-serif;
}
body {
  font-size: 92%;
}
#nav {
  margin: 0;
  padding: 0;
  background: #6F6146;
  list-style-type: none;
  width: 180px;
  float: left; /* Contain floated list items */
}
#nav li {
  margin: 0;
  padding: 0;
  float: left; /* This corrects the */
  width: 100%; /* IE whitespace bug */
}
#nav a {
  display: block;  /* to increase clickable area as a's
      default to inline */
  color: #FFF;
  text-decoration: none;
  padding: 0 15px;
  line-height: 2.5;
  border-bottom: 1px solid #FFF;
}
#nav #nav_con a {
  border: none;
}
#nav a:hover {
  background: #4F4532;
}
#body_hom #nav_hom a,
    #body_map #nav_map a,#body_jou #nav_jou a,
    #body_his #nav_his a,#body_ref #nav_ref a,
    #body_con #nav_con a {
  background: #BEB06F;
  color: #1A1303;
  font-weight: bold;
}
```

You should see something similar to Figure 4.5 when you view your work in a browser.

Figure 4.5: Combined style sheet and markup

Basic Horizontal Navigation

We've ensured that our vertical navigation is solid, working properly, and semantically correct. We're not out of the woods just yet, though. Our designer friend contacts us, wringing his hands in dismay and frustration, just as we sit down for a well-earned drink. Now it turns out that the client wants the navigation to display as a horizontal bar across the top of the page. The designer gives us a new mockup for the navigation element, which is pictured in Figure 4.6.

Figure 4.6: Mockup for horizontal navigation

Fortunately, there's a strong similarity between the new navigation mockup and our existing styled version. However, let's note the clear differences in the new version:

- It's obviously much wider than the vertical navigation.
- The text is centered in each list item, and the list item itself is not as wide as before.
- Most obviously, the items are beside each other, not stacked on top of one another.

There's not a great deal to be changed in our existing CSS:

- We need to alter the width of the unordered list element to the new size; the list items no longer need a **width** of **100%** now that they're beside one another.
- The anchor element will incur the most changes. It no longer needs a **block display** because the element will be floated.
- Since we aren't declaring any margins here, we don't need to worry about the IE double-margin bug.
- As we're centering the text, the left and right **padding** can be deleted, and the **border** will move to the right, not the bottom.

Let's see those changes in code:

horizontal.css (excerpt)

```css
#nav {
  margin: 0;
  padding: 0;
  background: #6F6146;
  list-style-type: none;
  width: 767px;
  float: left; /* Contain floated list items */
}
#nav li {
  margin: 0;
  padding: 0;
  float: left;
}
#nav a {
  float: left;
  width: 127px;
  text-align: center;
  color: #FFF;
  text-decoration: none;
  line-height: 2.5;
  border-right: 1px solid #FFF;
}
```

Let's take a look at the page in our various browsers to see how they render the new styles. The displays are shown in Figure 4.7. Remember, our markup hasn't changed at all, and neither has much of our style sheet. The code above only replaces the specific styles that were declared for our vertical navigation styles. The remainder of the styles are left intact.

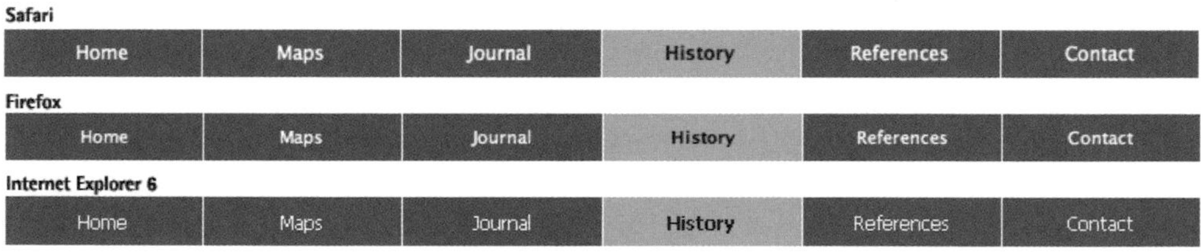

Figure 4.7: Checking initial changes across Safari, Firefox, and Internet Explorer

Great! Our hover styles are still working properly, as is the You Are Here navigation. This is a perfect example of the power of CSS: we make no changes to the markup, six changes to the style sheet, and our navigation is completely altered! Let's inspect the completed style sheet for our horizontal navigation:

horizontal.css (excerpt)

```css
html {
    font: small/1.4 "Lucida Grande", Tahoma, sans-serif;
}
body {
    font-size: 92%;
}
#nav {
  margin: 0;
  padding: 0;
  background: #6F6146;
  list-style-type: none;
  width: 767px;
  float: left; /* Contain floated list items */
}
#nav li {
  margin: 0;
  padding: 0;
  float: left;
}
#nav a {
  float: left;
  width: 127px;
  color: #FFF;
  text-decoration: none;
  line-height: 2.5;
  text-align: center;
  border-right: 1px solid #FFF;
}
#nav #nav_con a {
  border: none;
}
#nav a:hover {
  background: #4F4532;
}
#body_hom #nav_hom a, #body_map #nav_map a,
    #body_jou #nav_jou a,#body_his #nav_his a,
    #body_ref #nav_ref a,
    #body_con #nav_con a {
  background: #BEB06F;
  color: #1A1303;
  font-weight: bold;
}
```

The change from vertical to horizontal navigation has been a complete success—without causing too much of a headache. It must be time to send our work off to the designer, and relax with that drink!

Tabbed Navigation

No—sorry. If you thought we were finished, think again! Over the weekend, our client went shopping online for DVDs at Amazon.com, and noticed those nice tabs that offer horizontal navigation to *x* gazillion daily Amazon site visitors. He's decided that if those tabs are good enough for Amazon, they'll be good enough for Cartography Corner, and he wants us to redesign the navigation *again*. It seems an irksome chore for the moment, but remain calm: in most circumstances, tabs are very simple to implement. Only under a few scenarios, which we'll discuss later on, do they present more of an issue. But let's first take a look at implementing tabs within our existing navigation.

Each list item in our menu is the same width, so turning our existing navigation items into tabs is quite easy. We'll just apply a single image to each of our tabs, and keep using the same hover styles and current behavior—we don't need any additional markup. As before, we'll start with our designer's mockup, which looks like Figure 4.8.

Figure 4.8: Initial design for tabbed navigation

This looks very similar to the previous navigation design, except that the top corners of each menu item are now rounded. As there's no good way to round those corners using CSS styles alone, we'll have to rely on images to accomplish this effect. We note that there are three distinct colors, so it makes sense that we'll need three different tab images to create our menu.

If we leave the tabs as separate images, however, the browser will not load the hover tab graphic when the page is initially loaded in the user's browser. As the user begins to hover over the navigation, that image will be loaded in the background. The user will see a darkened background color, but the image of the rounded corners will drop into place only after the page has finished loading. This is definitely not the behavior we want to see!

Ideally, the browser would load all three tab states when the page loads, so as to avoid any undesired display issues arising from the loading behavior. When I think about pre-loading images, I immediately recall using JavaScript to load hidden image objects, like I used to do back in 1999. These days, the power of CSS offers us a much cleaner, more elegant solution.

Applying Tab Images

Instead of creating three separate images for the tab states, let's try combining all three states into a single image. That way, all three states will be loaded at the same time, and we'll simply select the state we need by moving the `background-image` around with the CSS `background-position` property. As the `width` of the tab is defined for this menu, we'll put the three states side by side into a single image like the one shown in Figure 4.9.

Figure 4.9: Our normal, active, and hover tab states combined into one image

If we look at the styles we created for the previous horizontal menu, a `width` is specified for each anchor, so each state of the tab image needs to be the same width. When the image is placed in the background of the anchor, only that part of the image that fits within the defined width and height of the element will be rendered—the rest will remain hidden. Let's use this fact to our advantage as we make a few modifications to our styles to add the tab graphic. I've saved the image in a directory named *images* alongside the style sheet, and named it `tab.gif`:

fixed-tabs.css (excerpt)

```
#nav a {
  float: left;
  width: 127px;
  color: #FFF;
  text-decoration: none"
  line-height: 2.5;
  text-align: center;
  border-right: 1px solid #FFF;
  background: url(images/tab.gif) no-repeat;
}
```

That's it. One single line, and our image file turns our blocky horizontal menu items into tabs, as shown in Figure 4.10.

Figure 4.10: Tab image applied to horizontal menu

But look at Figure 4.11—this is what happens when we mouse over the menu items!

Figure 4.11: Tabs disappearing on hover

Our tab image seems to have disappeared; our rounded corners have vanished, to be replaced by our old sharp ones. This effect is the result of our declaring the `background` property on our hover style, which sets the color correctly but overwrites the `background-image` part of the `background` declaration. However, if we specify the `background-color`, the `background-image` will inherit as it should. Here's what that looks like:

```
                                           fixed-tabs.css (excerpt)
#nav a:hover {
  background-color: #4F4532;
}
```

We also need to change the color of the tab image. To do so, we shift the background image to the left in order to align our hover state image properly inside the element frame:

```
#nav a:hover {
  background-color: #4F4532;
  background-position: -127px 0;
}
```

This is where the `background-position` property comes into play—it's illustrated in Figure 4.12. We need to shift the background image to the left by the exact `width` of the anchor element—127px in our case.

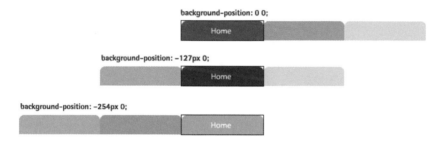

Figure 4.12: Shifting the background image for hover, active, and normal states

NOTE   Background Positioning

When setting the `background-position` property, the order of the two values is very important. The first represents horizontal movement, the second defines vertical movement. We can use positive or negative values like **35px** or **-2em**, or text descriptions like **top**, **bottom**, **left**, or **right**.

If we test our code now, we'll see that our hover state is working as it should. Figure 4.13 shows that we're back on track.

Figure 4.13: Successful `background-image` shift

Activating the "You Are Here" State

Now all that's left for us to do is to activate the You Are Here state on the navigation. We take the same approach to this step as we did to our hover state, only this time we move the background an additional 127px to the left:

fixed-tabs.css (excerpt)

```
#body_hom #nav_hom a,#body_map #nav_map a,#body_jou #nav_jou a,
   #body_his #nav_his a,#body_ref #nav_ref a,
   #body_con #nav_con a {
  background-color: #BEB06F;
  background-position: -254px 0;
  color: #1A1303;
  font-weight: bold;
}
```

Refreshing the browser should now show the completed navigation, as in Figure 4.14.

Figure 4.14: Completed tab navigation, showing hover state and "You Are Here" state

If we view our menu in all browsers, we'll see that no further adjustments need to be made. Let's take a look at the final style sheet:

fixed-tabs.css

```
html {
  font: small/1.4 "Lucida Grande", Tahoma, sans-serif;
}
body {
  font-size: 92%;
}
#nav {
  margin: 0;
  padding: 0;
  background: #6F6146;
  list-style-type: none;
  width: 767px;
  float: left;
}
#nav li {
  margin: 0;
  padding: 0;
  float: left;
}
```

```
#nav a {
  float: left;
  width: 127px;
  color: #FFF;
  text-decoration: none;
  line-height: 2.5;
  text-align: center;
  border-right: 1px solid #FFF;
  background: url(images/tab.gif) no-repeat;
}
#nav #nav_con a {
  border: none;
}
#nav a:hover {
  background-color: #4F4532;
  background-position: -127px 0;
}
#body_hom #nav_hom a,#body_map #nav_map a,
   #body_jou #nav_jou a,#body_his #nav_his a,
   #body_ref #nav_ref a,#body_con #nav_con a {
  background-color: #BEB06F;
  background-position: -254px 0;
  color: #1A1303;
  font-weight: bold;
}
```

NOTE   *Keeping your Styles Simple*

While not navigation-specific, it's often very helpful to remember that when it comes to markup and styles, it's the simple, standard solutions that yield the best and most consistent results. If, in trying to get a feature to work, you keep adding markup and styles, and trying all sorts of weird hacks and advanced CSS methods, you're probably best starting over from scratch. There's nothing like clearing the canvas to highlight the most obvious solutions.

Variable-width Tabs

Now, this menu is all well and good, but it does require the anchors to be all the same width.

But what if you want them to be sized relative to the text they contain? Well, that situation presents a few other issues, not least of them being that it puts us in a position of having to choose between implementing a design behavior and using minimal markup.

Let's explore these variable-width tabs. We'll start with the markup we developed in the previous section but, in order to use it, we'll have to take advantage of the styling hooks offered by the list items themselves. So far, we've simply pushed the styling hooks out of the way, but now we'll have to incorporate them as a fully fledged part of our menu.

The basic concept here is to put the `background-color` and `border` properties on the list item, and apply one corner of the tab as a `background-image` on one side. The contained anchor will have a transparent `background` except for the other corner image on the opposite side. We'll float the list item and the anchor to make them both shrink their `width` values to suit the size of the contained text.

Applying Tab Images

Let's start by creating our images, which can be conceptualized as being something like those shown in Figure 4.15. They only need to be as large as the whitespace created by the corner of the tab. We'll need one for each corner, and, for now, we'll only concentrate on the default state of the navigation items. It's important to note that the white corners of the tabs should be completely opaque, so as to cover up the background color of the list items. Transparency is not needed for this effect, and in reality, it just won't work with the way we're styling the menu.

Figure 4.15: The corner pieces of our variable-width tabs

Let's start work on the markup. I'll start with a clean style sheet for ease of explanation:

variable-tabs.css (excerpt)

```
html {
  font: small/1.4 "Lucida Grande", Tahoma, sans-serif;
}
body {
  font-size: 92%;
}
#nav {
  margin: 0;
  padding: 0;
  list-style-type: none;
  float: left;
}
```

```
#nav li {
  margin: 0;
  padding: 0;
  float: left;
  margin: 0 1px 0 0;
  display: inline;
  background: #6F6146 url(images/tab_left.gif) no-repeat;
}
#nav a {
  float: left;
  padding: 0 15px;
  color: #FFF;
  text-decoration: none;
  line-height: 2.5;
  background: url(images/tab_right.gif) no-repeat top right;
}
```

NOTE   *Default Background Positioning*

You may notice that in the **#nav li** style, I don't specify any position on the **background** property, while on the **#nav a**, I specify a position of **top right**. This approach is used simply because when no **background-position** is specified, the property defaults to the **top left**, or **0 0**.

The **html** and **body** declarations are, once again, simply used to define a **font** and **font-size** for our example. In a real-world project, these values should match your design's font specifications. If you look at the **#nav** properties, you'll notice that we no longer have a **width** defined. This omission is completely optional, although if your navigation needs to fit into a specific **width**, I would recommend declaring that value here, just to be sure. Also, if you plan to have the **background** on the **#nav** element stretch past the list items (assuming they don't take up the entire width of the **background**), you'll have to define a **width** here. Other than that, the simple declarations in the code above float the element, strip any **margin**s and **padding**, and remove the list styles.

For the menu items, we strip **margin**s and **padding** and float each **li**. Floating the elements causes them to scale horizontally to their contained content, which is the aim of our variable-width tab. A **margin** of 1px is applied to the right of the list item to visually separate the tabs from each other. This **margin** can be increased or removed to meet your design specifications. If the **margin** is anything other than zero, the **display** property needs to be set to **inline** to correct the IE double-margin bug.[6] Lastly, we apply the default **background-color**, and cover up the top-left corner with our *tab_left.gif* image.

---

6   http://www.positioniseverything.net/explorer/doubled-margin.html

We float our anchor element inside the list item. This step automatically turns the link into an **inline-block**, so the declaring of properties like **padding** and **background** will work as expected, and it will shrink horizontally to fit the text inside the element.[7] The left and right **padding** of **15px** can be modified to your design needs, along with the **color**, **text-decoration**, and **line-height** properties. Finally, we cover up the top right of the tab with our *top_right.gif* image to complete the tab effect. Let's see what we have so far—take a look at Figure 4.16.

Figure 4.16: A first look at our variable-width tabs

Applying Hover Styles

Now we can apply our hover styles. In the previous examples, we changed the whole tab color on hover. But in this example, the **background-color** isn't on the anchor element, it's on the parent list item. Until Internet Explorer 6 is fully replaced by IE 7, this presents a major issue in that we can't access the **hover** pseudo-class on anything but the anchor element. IE 7 will support the **hover** pseudo-class on any element, but IE 6 and earlier do not. Consequently, we can't change any of the list item's properties by hovering over it in IE 6. Also, because we're using a background on the list item behind the anchor, we can't put a background color on the anchor itself, as it will cover up the list item's background image.

As I mentioned before, this method may require you to choose between using the styling hooks in a complex design, and your desire for simplified markup. If we really need to change the whole tab color using this method and have it work in IE 6, then we need to place inside each anchor an additional element that wraps around the contained text; usually this element is something like a **span**:

```
<li id="nav_hom"><a href="/"><span>Home</span></a></li>
```

While this is possible, it adds non-semantic markup to the page, and requires the list item styles to be applied to the anchor and **span** instead of the list item itself. Let's consider changing our design requirements so that on hover, we simply change the navigation item's text **color**. Let's try this—you can see the results in Figure 4.17:

variable-tabs.css (excerpt)

```
#nav a:hover {
  color: #F90;
}
```

---

7   http://www.w3.org/TR/CSS21/visuren.html#display-prop

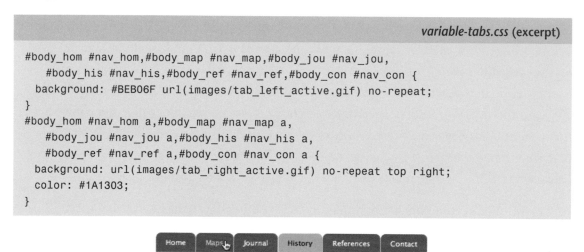

Figure 4.17: Changing the text color only for the hover state

Adding the "You Are Here" State

After checking with our designer, we decide that changing the menu item's text color is an acceptable way to indicate a link in our navigation, and we can move on to create the You Are Here states. We're using the list item to indicate which menu item is currently being used, so it's no problem to create an additional set of tab images for the You Are Here state, and simply activate those as we have the previous You Are Here styles. These current state tab images will be identical to the default state, except for their colors, as Figure 4.18 shows:

variable-tabs.css (excerpt)

```
#body_hom #nav_hom,#body_map #nav_map,#body_jou #nav_jou,
   #body_his #nav_his,#body_ref #nav_ref,#body_con #nav_con {
  background: #BEB06F url(images/tab_left_active.gif) no-repeat;
}
#body_hom #nav_hom a,#body_map #nav_map a,
   #body_jou #nav_jou a,#body_his #nav_his a,
   #body_ref #nav_ref a,#body_con #nav_con a {
  background: url(images/tab_right_active.gif) no-repeat top right;
  color: #1A1303;
}
```

Figure 4.18: Variable-width tabs showing You Are Here state

Now the tabs will adjust to the size of the text they contain; we've also activated acceptable **hover** and You Are Here states. Let's see all the styles together:

variable-tabs.css

```
html {
  font: small/1.4 "Lucida Grande", Tahoma, sans-serif;
}
body {
  font-size: 92%;
}#nav {
  margin: 0;
  padding: 0;
  list-style-type: none;
  float: left;
}
```

```
#nav li {
  margin: 0;
  padding: 0;
  float: left;
  margin: 0 1px 0 0;
  display: inline;
  background: #6F6146 url(images/tab_left.gif) no-repeat;
}
#nav a {
  float: left;
  padding: 0 15px;
  color: #FFF;
  text-decoration: none;
  line-height: 2.5;
   background: url(images/tab_right.gif) no-repeat top right;
}
#nav a:hover {
  color: #F90;
}
#body_hom #nav_hom,#body_map #nav_map,#body_jou #nav_jou,
    #body_his #nav_his,#body_ref #nav_ref,#body_con #nav_con {
  background: #BEB06F url(images/tab_left_active.gif) no-repeat;
}
#body_hom #nav_hom a,#body_map #nav_map a,#body_jou #nav_jou a,
    #body_his #nav_his a,#body_ref #nav_ref a,
    #body_con #nav_con a {
  background: url(images/tab_right_active.gif) no-repeat
     top right;
  color: #1A1303;
}
```

This method of styling tabs works very well for menus that don't make heavy use of graphical textures or backgrounds.

Next, we'll explore an approach to styling a very graphic-intense navigation system.[8]

---

8   An alternate method for menus that make heavy use of backgrounds is presented by Doug Bowman of StopDesign in his article "Sliding Doors of CSS," October 20, 2003, http://www.alistapart.com/articles/slidingdoors/.

Advanced Horizontal Navigation

After our diversion into tabbed navigation, we return to our project only to find that our client's thrown us another curve ball. He's had a perfunctory look at all our hard work, and, instead of showering us with the praise we deserve, he's issued yet another request to change things. Here's his feedback:

> The navigation looks too plain. We have to use the company font—no substitutions. And there needs to be some sort of graphical background. And drop shadows. Every good web site uses drop shadows.

A few hours later, after the designer has managed to overcome his pique with plenty of chamomile tea and breathing exercises, he presents us with a mockup for the new navigation.

Figure 4.19: New navigation design, using company font and drop shadows

This design has some definite issues that present several challenges:

- As the designer has chosen a font that we can't expect the majority of users to have in their browsers, and included a drop shadow, we'll have to use image replacement techniques instead of live text.
- The list items are no longer all the same `width`.
- The hover and You Are Here states have specific `background-color`s and images.

We'll use the **navigation matrix** technique to deal with the challenges posed by image replacement and multiple states—a method originally posted at Superfluous Banter.[9] The navigation matrix uses a single image and a combination of styles to turn an unordered list into an image-replaced menu. This technique works by shifting the single image around the various list items using the `background-position` property. This ensures that the exact part of the image that represents the item and its state will be displayed.

An added benefit of using a single image in the navigation is that it provides immediate response on hover; there's no delay for the user while their browser loads the hover state images.

Creating Navigation Matrix

Let's start by creating the image that will form the basis of our matrix. The graphic provided by the designer is 767px wide, and 30px tall. In order to create our image, we

---

9   http://superfluousbanter.org/archives/2004/05/navigation-matrix/

need each item to be rendered separately in each state: normal, hover, and You Are Here. The `width` of our main image will stay at 767px, but to accommodate all three states, we'll triple the `height` to 90px and include each state in the graphic. The finished product will look like Figure 4.20.

Figure 4.20: Our matrix image

We'll save it as *menu.jpg*, in a folder named *images*, in the same parent folder as our style sheet.

Our using this image replacement ensures that the menu is a fixed width—it won't resize to fit any changes in the length of the list item text, so we'll always know the exact dimensions of the navigation as a whole, as well as those of each list item. For this reason, absolutely positioning the list items will serve us well. As support for absolute positioning is very well established in modern browsers, absolute positioning will allow easy control of the positioning of the tabs without problems of browser incompatibility. The positioning of the list items doesn't *have* to be done absolutely, but it does represent the easiest positioning method for the purposes of this demonstration.

Applying Some Styles

Let's style the unordered list element as we did in the vertical navigation:

advanced-tabs.css (excerpt)

```
#nav {
  width: 767px;
  height: 30px;
  position: relative;
  background: url(images/menu.jpg);
  margin: 0;
  padding: 0;
}
```

The unordered list is positioned relatively so that we have a base with which to position the anchors. We give the list a `background` of the menu item to help eliminate an issue that sometimes arises with Internet Explorer. Occasionally, when a user mouses over a menu item, IE will briefly drop the `background-image` while repositioning it. With no image behind the menu item, some IE users would see a flash of white (or whatever `background` was behind the unordered list) when hovering over the menu. By specifying `background-image` on the unordered list, we ensure that even if IE does drop the image for a split second on positioning, the graphic duplicated on the menu behind will show through, thus eliminating the flash.

We'll need to use a small amount of arithmetic when styling the anchor elements, in order to accurately position them and their backgrounds. The exact position of each anchor needs to be calculated so we know where to place it within the unordered list, and how to reposition the `background-image` into its correct location, as illustrated in Figure 4.21.

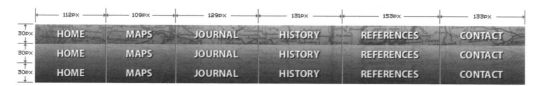

Figure 4.21: Working out **background-position** for different states

Let's take full advantage of the individual list item **id** attribute in order to style and position each list item's anchor element. First, we'll style the list items to make sure they stay inside the unordered list. Next, we'll generically style the anchor elements with every style that will be shared across them. Finally, we'll specify the unique styles for each element:

advanced-tabs.css (excerpt)

```css
#nav li {
  float: left;
}
#nav li a {
  position: absolute;
  top: 0;
  margin: 0;
  padding: 0;
  display: block;
  height: 30px;
  background: url(images/menu.jpg) no-repeat;
  text-indent: -9999px;
  overflow: hidden;
  font-size: 1%;
}
li#nav_hom a {
  left: 0;
  width: 112px;
  background-position: 0 0;
}
li#nav_map a {
  left: 112px;
  width: 109px;
  background-position: -112px 0;
}
```

```
li#nav_jou a {
  left: 221px;
  width: 129px;
  background-position: -221px 0;
}
li#nav_his a {
  left: 350px;
  width: 131px;
  background-position: -350px 0;
}
li#nav_ref a {
  left: 481px;
  width: 153px;
  background-position: -481px 0;
}
li#nav_con a {
  left: 634px;
  width: 133px;
  background-position: -634px 0;
}
```

Clearly, we've set each anchor with a specific **width**, a **height** of 30px, and positioned it to its exact location using the **left** property. As all the menu anchor elements share the same **background-image**—*menu.jpg*—we need to move the **background-image** back to the left to display the image in the correct position. It makes sense that we move the **background-image** the same distance to the left as we moved the anchor to the right.

In a browser (or Figure 4.22), it's evident that the navigation works in the default state, and that all the anchors are in their correct locations and have the proper **background-position**.

Figure 4.22: First look at our new navigation

Activating the Hover States

Now to activate the hover states! You can see from the You Are Here styles that we're moving the background image to the left, but are leaving it positioned at the top of its parent list item.

To activate the hovers, all we need to do is move the **background-image** up by the exact height of the menu; in this case, 30px:

advanced-tabs.css (excerpt)

```
li#nav_hom a:hover {
  background-position: 0 -30px;
}
```

```css
li#nav_map a:hover {
  background-position: -112px -30px;
}
li#nav_jou a:hover {
  background-position: -221px -30px;
}
li#nav_his a:hover {
  background-position: -350px -30px;
}
li#nav_ref a:hover {
  background-position: -481px -30px;
}
li#nav_con a:hover {
  background-position: -634px -30px;
}
```

With these styles in place, we can test the page in the browser to ensure that the hover states are activated. Our display looks good in Figure 4.23.

Figure 4.23: Navigation matrix with hover styles

Lastly, we activate the You Are Here state on the navigation items. We manage this by again utilizing the **id** attribute on the **body** element, and associating it with a specific list item **id**. We'll shift the **background-image** up just as we did with the hover states, except that this time we'll move it up another 30px, for a total of 60px:

advanced-tabs.css (excerpt)

```css
#body_hom li#nav_hom  a {
  background-position: 0 -60px;
}
#body_map li#nav_map a {
  background-position: -112px -60px;
}
#body_jou li#nav_jou a {
  background-position: -221px -60px;
}
#body_his li#nav_his a {
  background-position: -350px -60px;
}
#body_ref li#nav_ref a {
  background-position: -481px -60px;
}
#body_con li#nav_con a {
  background-position: -634px -60px;
}
```

Reload the page in the browser, and you'll see that the added styles correctly activate the You Are Here state. Figure 4.24 shows how the navigation displays in all the browsers we're using.

Figure 4.24: Testing the final menu for cross-browser compatibility

As you can see, this method produces exactly the same look across all browsers. From a design standpoint, using images to create the entire navigation allows us to most closely recreate the designer's mockup. We only use established CSS methods, so we don't encounter many browser quirks. We do sacrifice some aspects of the navigation's usability, such as the ability to resize text; also, the styles rely on images, so if the images are disabled in a user's browser, the user will be confronted with nothing but a blank white strip where the navigation elements should be. As always, make sure these limitations are acceptable for your specific project before committing to this style of navigation.

Let's put all these styles together to see what our completed navigation style sheet looks like:

advanced-tabs.css

```css
#nav {
  width: 767px;
  height: 30px;
  position: relative;
  background: url(images/menu.jpg);
  margin: 0;
  padding: 0;
}
#nav li {
  float: left;
}
```

```
#nav li a {
  position: absolute;
  top: 0;
  margin: 0;
  padding: 0;
  display: block;
  height: 30px;
  background: url(images/menu.jpg) no-repeat;
  text-indent: -9999px;
  overflow: hidden;
  font-size: 1%;
}
li#nav_hom a {
  left: 0;
  width: 112px;
  background-position: 0 0;
}
li#nav_map a {
  left: 112px;
  width: 109px;
  background-position: -112px 0;
}
li#nav_jou a {
  left: 221px;
  width: 129px;
  background-position: -221px 0;
}
li#nav_his a {
  left: 350px;
  width: 131px;
  background-position: -350px 0;
}
li#nav_ref a {
  left: 481px;
  width: 153px;
  background-position: -481px 0;
}
li#nav_con  a {
  left: 634px;
  width: 133px;
  background-position: -634px 0;
}
li#nav_hom a:hover {
  background-position: 0 -30px;
}
li#nav_map a:hover {
  background-position: -112px -30px;
}
```

```
li#nav_jou a:hover {
  background-position: -221px -30px;
}
li#nav_his a:hover {
  background-position: -350px -30px;
}
li#nav_ref a:hover {
  background-position: -481px -30px;
}
li#nav_con a:hover {
  background-position: -634px -30px;
}
#body_hom li#nav_hom  a {
  background-position: 0 -60px;
}
#body_map li#nav_map a {
  background-position: -112px -60px;
}
#body_jou li#nav_jou a {
  background-position: -221px -60px;
}
#body_his li#nav_his a {
  background-position: -350px -60px;
}
#body_ref li#nav_ref a {
  background-position: -481px -60px;
}
#body_con li#nav_con a {
  background-position: -634px -60px;
}
```

WARNING   *Finalize, then Stylize*

If you decide to use a navigation matrix, be very sure that the design and copy for your navigation is complete before you dive into the CSS. The navigation matrix method is very powerful, and relatively simple to implement, but it's a real pain to edit. You basically have to undertake the whole journey again each time there's a change—even if it's only a 1px shift of an anchor—so finalize that design before you begin to apply the styles.

The client takes one look at our navigation efforts, and a huge grin spreads across his face. Finally, he's happy. It's taken a long time and a lot of changes to please this fussy client, but we've successfully delivered the navigation menu he's always wanted. All's well that ends well!

Summary

Navigation is key to the success of a web site, and integral to both its identity and usability. As you can see from the examples we've covered in this chapter, it's not difficult to achieve a great-looking navigation menu with CSS, which also gives us plenty of freedom in terms of how we style navigation elements.

In this chapter, we've worked together to create the navigation for a simulated project, from establishing the basic markup, to creating advanced vertical and horizontal navigation menus, as well as tabbed and variable-width navigation systems. We've encountered some problems, but resolved them with our careful application of styling. Of course, we've only touched on the most useful few of many possible courses of action in this chapter, and all of these exercises can be built upon to create new and different navigation menus.

Remember: the raison d'être of navigation is to help users find whatever they're looking for quickly and efficiently. Above all, navigation must be obvious and simple. Creativity and usability must work together to create a functional balance between freedom and consistency. Styling the elements is just one step in the process—but I hope it's now an easier one!

Forms

Contact Form

Fields marked with * are required.

Name

E-mail address

Message*

Mai

Forms. Is there any other word that strikes as much fear into the hearts of grown web designers?

I think that the reputation of forms as an untamable, ugly necessity has arisen for two reasons:

- Form elements arc derived from native operating system widgets, which makes them particularly difficult to style.
- Forms are often critical to the function of a web site— they're most often employed as search boxes, inquiry forms, or shopping cart checkouts—and need to function as smoothly as possible in order to meet user expectations.

However, it's still possible to incorporate both these points into designing a form tailored to the style of the rest of your site. This chapter will explore the ways in which you can design a great-looking form, and provide you with the necessary code, which we'll work work through together.

Element Subgroups

Fill in your details below. We promise that we won't use them to spam you with advertisements ... much.

Contact Details

Name:

Occupation:
   ☐ Doctor

   ☐ Lawyer

   ☐ Teacher

   ☐ Web designer

Telephone:

Accessible Form Markup

Before we can begin to look at form layout, we need to craft some really solid markup that will provide us with a framework to which we can add some style.

Forms represent the one area of your web site where you absolutely *must* commit time and energy to ensure user accessibility. Even though forms represent some of the most complex interactions that can occur on a web page, in many cases these interactions are only represented visually—via the proximity of a form element to its `label`, or grouping by borders and background colors. Users of assistive technology such as screen readers may not be able to see these visual clues, so it's vital that you support these users by ensuring accessibility. The key concept behind providing an accessible form is to have descriptive labeling of all its sections and `input` elements.

In particular, this means the proper usage of two elements: `label` and `legend`.

There's also an improperly held belief that the only way you can guarantee that a form displays properly is by using tables. All of the code reproduced here for forms is standards-based, semantic markup, so you've got no excuse for relying on tables now!

Labeling Form Elements

No matter how you style a form element and its `label`, it generally conforms to a certain pattern:

- the form element itself
- a text label for the element
- a connection between the element and its textual description

This connection is made either through visual alignment, visual grouping, or some other visual indicator. In Figure 5.1, you can see that the form on the left makes a connection between the field element and its label purely through alignment, whereas the form on the right indicates a more explicit connection via the use of color.

Figure 5.1: Visual connections in forms

When accommodating users of assistive technology in the creation of your forms, there's one main question to consider. How can a user who's unable to see a web page create the connection between a form element and its text label, without the visual cues of proximity or grouping?

The answer is the **label** element. **label** is a special element applied to a form element to allow its textual description to be semantically linked to the element itself, so any assistive technology such as a screenreader can read out that text when it encounters its partner form element.

In order to use a **label**, wrap the textual description in a pair of **labellabel** tags, then add a **for** attribute to the **label**. The value of the **for** attribute should be the **id** of the form element with which you want to create a connection:

```
<label for="firstName">First name</label>
<input id="firstName" name="firstName" type="text" />
```

Now, when a screenreader encounters the **firstName** field, it'll also read out the text "First name" to the user, so he or she will know what to type into that field. The **label** doesn't have to be near the form element and neither of them have to be in any particular order—as long as the **label**'s **for** attribute contains a valid reference, the relationship will be understood. However, having the **label** right before the form element in the source order generally makes the most semantic sense.

A **label** should be applied to any form element that doesn't automatically include descriptive text, such as:

- checkboxes
- radio buttons
- **textarea**s
- text fields
- **select** boxes

Submit buttons and submit images don't require **label** elements, because their descriptions are contained, respectively, in their **value** and **alt** attributes.

Of course, you can easily style the text inside the **label** using CSS, so you can format the **label** text in your forms in the same way as if you were using a **span**, **p**, or **div**, but using a **label** has the benefit of being much more accessible than any of those elements.

Grouping Related Elements

legend goes hand in hand with **fieldset**. In fact, the only element of which a **legend** can be a child *is* a **fieldset**. A **fieldset** groups a series of related form elements. For instance, "street address," "suburb," "state," and "zip code" could all be grouped under "postal address." You could create a **fieldset** that groups all of those elements, and give it an appropriate **legend** to describe that group:

```
<form action="example.php">
  <fieldset>
    <legend>Postal Address</legend>
    <label for="street">Street address</label>
    <input id="street" name="street" type="text" />
    <label for=" suburb">Suburb</label>
    <input id="suburb" name="suburb" type="text" />
    <label for="state">State</label>
    <input id="state" name="state" type="text" />
    <label for="postcode">Postcode</label>
    <input id="postcode" name="postcode" type="text" />
  </fieldset>
</form>
```

Now that **legend** is associated with all those form elements inside the **fieldset**, when a person using a screenreader focuses on one of the form elements, the screenreader will also read out the **legend** text: "Postal Address; Suburb."

The benefit of the screenreader specifying both **legend** and **fieldset** becomes apparent when you have two groups of elements that are very similar, except for their group type:

```
<form action="example.php">
  <fieldset>
    <legend>Postal Address</legend>
    <label for="street">Street address</label>
    <input id="street" name="street" type="text" />
    <label for=" suburb">Suburb</label>
    <input id="suburb" name="suburb" type="text" />
    <label for="state">State</label>
    <input id="state" name="state" type="text" />
    <label for="postcode">Postcode</label>
    <input id="postcode" name="postcode" type="text" />
  </fieldset>
  <fieldset>
    <legend>Delivery Address</legend>
    <label for="deliveryStreet">Street address</label>
    <input id="deliveryStreet" name="deliveryStreet"
      type="text" />
    <label for="deliverySuburb">Suburb</label>
    <input id="deliverySuburb" name="deliverySuburb"
      type="text" />
    <label for="deliveryState">State</label>
    <input id="deliveryState" name="deliveryState"
      type="text" />
    <label for="deliveryPostcode">Postcode</label>
    <input id="deliveryPostcode" name="deliveryPostcode"
      type="text" />
  </fieldset>
</form>
```

As Figure 5.2 shows, with the **fieldset**'s **legend** elements in place it's quite easy to determine visually which fields fall under which group, even on an unstyled form.

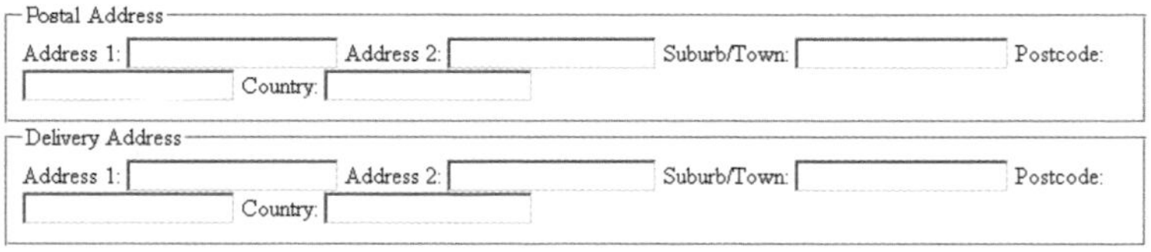

Figure 5.2: Unstyled form using **fieldset** and **legend** elements for grouping

But, you ask, couldn't the same visual effect be achieved using **h1** elements instead of **legend** elements?

Yes. However, the point of using **legend** is that without proper semantic grouping and labeling, a screenreader user would become confused as to why he or she was required to enter "Address 1" twice. With the **legend** included, the user will know that the second "Address 1" actually belongs to another group—the group for the delivery address.

So, by combining **label** and **legend**, we give visually impaired users the ability to navigate and fill in our forms much more easily. By using this combination as the basic structure for your forms, you'll ensure that not only will they look fantastic, but they'll be accessible as well!

Form Layout

There are several different ways in which you can lay out a form. The method you choose depends upon how long the form is, its purpose, how often it will be used by each person who has to fill it out, and, of course, the general aesthetics of the web page.

It's generally considered most efficient to have one form element per line, with the lines stacked sequentially one on top of the other, as most Western-language web pages are designed to scroll vertically rather than horizontally. This allows users to follow the path to completion easily and focus their attention on entering one piece of data at a time.

For each form element in a left-to-right reading system, it's logical to position the corresponding **label** in one of three ways:

- directly above the form element
- in a separate left column, left-aligned
- in a separate left column, right-aligned

Each of these approaches has its own advantages and its own look, so consider these options when you're deciding how to lay out a form for a particular page.

Labels that are positioned directly above a form element have been shown to be processed most quickly by users. The compact grouping between label and element reduces eye movement by allowing the user to observe both simultaneously.[1] However, this type of positioning is rather utilitarian, and isn't the most aesthetically pleasing layout. It also has the disadvantage of occupying the most vertical space of the three layouts, which will make a long form even longer. Generally, top-positioned labels work well for short forms that are familiar to the user, such as the comment form in Figure 5.3.

Figure 5.3: Labels positioned above form elements[2]

Labels that are positioned in a column to the left of the elements look much more organized and neat, but the way in which the text in those labels is aligned also affects the usability of the form.

Right-aligning the text creates a much stronger grouping between the label and the element. However, the ragged left edge of the labels can make the form look messy and reduces the ability of users to scan the labels by themselves.[3] In a left-aligned column, the labels instantly become easier to scan, but their grouping with the associated form elements becomes weaker. Users have to spend a little more time correlating the labels with their elements, resulting in slower form completion. An example of left-aligned labels can be seen in Figure 5.4.

1   http://www.uxmatters.com/MT/archives/000107.php
2   http://dressfordialogue.com/thoughts/chris-cornell/
3   http://www.lukew.com/resources/articles/web_forms.html

Figure 5.4: Labels positioned in a column and aligned left[4]

The right-aligned column layout shown in Figure 5.5 allows for quicker association between label and element, so again it's more appropriate for forms that will be visited repeatedly by the user. Both layouts have the advantage of occupying a minimal amount of vertical space.

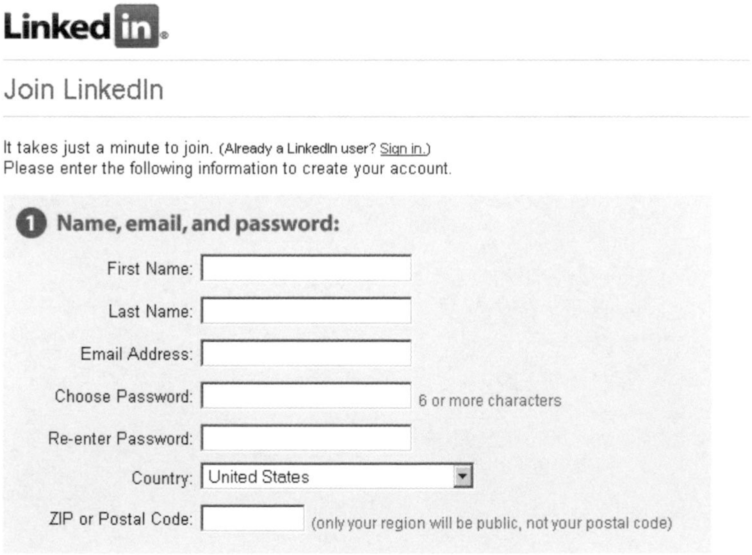

Figure 5.5: Labels positioned in a column and aligned right[5]

4   http://www.themaninblue.com/contact/
5   https://www.linkedin.com/register/

Using the CSS

To create each of these different types of `form` layouts, we'll use identical markup, but with different CSS rules.

In our example, the HTML looks like this:

```
<form action="example.php">
  <fieldset>
    <legend>Contact Details</legend>
    <ol>
      <li>
        <label for="name">Name:</label>
        <input id="name" name="name" class="text" type="text" />
      </li>
      <li>
        <label for="email">Email address:</label>
        <input id="email" name="email" class="text" type="text" />
      </li>
      <li>
        <label for="phone">Telephone:</label>
        <input id="phone" name="phone" class="text" type="text" />
      </li>
    </ol>
  </fieldset>
  <fieldset>
    <legend>Delivery Address</legend>
    <ol>
      <li>
        <label for="address1">Address 1:</label>
        <input id="address1" name="address1" class="text"
           type="text" />
      </li>
      <li>
        <label for="address2">Address 2:</label>
        <input id="address2" name="address2" class="text"
           type="text" />
      </li>
      <li>
        <label for="suburb">Suburb/Town:</label>
        <input id="suburb" name="suburb" class="text"
           type="text" />
      </li>
      <li>
        <label for="postcode">Postcode:</label>
        <input id="postcode" name="postcode"
           class="text textSmall" type="text" />
      </li>
```

```
      <li>
        <label for="country">Country:</label>
        <input id="country" name="country" class="text"
            type="text" />
      </li>
    </ol>


  </fieldset>
  <fieldset class="submit">
    <input class="submit" type="submit"
        value="Begin download" />
  </fieldset>
</form>
```

This HTML uses exactly the same `fieldset-legend-label` structure that we saw earlier in this chapter. However, you should see one glaring addition: inside the `fieldset` elements is an ordered list whose list items wrap around each of the form element/label pairs that we're using.

The reason for this addition? We need some extra markup in order to allow for all of the styling that we'll do to our forms in this chapter. There are just not enough styling hooks in the standard `fieldset-label` structure to allow us to provide robust borders, background colors, and column alignment.

There are a number of superfluous elements that we could add to the form that would grant us the extra styling hooks. We could move the form elements inside their `label` elements and wrap the `label` text in a `span`, or wrap a `div` around each form element/label pair. However, none of those choices would really contribute anything to the markup other than its presence.

The beauty of using an ordered list is that it adds an extra level of semantics to the structure of the form, and also makes the form display quite well in the absence of styles (say, on legacy browsers such as Netscape 4, or even simple mobile devices).

With no CSS applied and without the ordered lists, the rendered markup would appear as in Figure 5.6.

Figure 5.6: Unstyled form without any superfluous markup

Figure 5.7 shows how the unstyled form looks when we include the ordered lists.

Extra Form Markup

Fill in your details below. We promise that we won't use them to spam you with advertisements ... much.

Contact Details
1. Name:
2. Email address:
3. Telephone:

Delivery Address
1. Address 1:
2. Address 2:
3. Suburb/Town:
4. Postcode:
5. Country:

Begin download

Figure 5.7: Unstyled form that includes an ordered list inside each fieldset

I'm sure you'll agree that the version of the form that includes ordered lists is much easier to follow, and hence fill out.

> **NOTE Using Lists in Forms**
>
> If you're vehemently opposed to the inclusion of an ordered list inside your form markup, you can easily substitute it for some other wrapper element; all you need is one extra container around each form element/label pair in order to style your forms any way you want.

Two other HTML oddities that you might have picked up on:

- Each form **input** has a **class** that replicates its **type** attribute, for example **class="text" type="text"**. If you need to style a form element, this is a handy way of accessing it, given that Internet Explorer 6 and earlier don't support CSS attribute selectors (although Internet Explorer 7 does, so you mightn't need to include these extra classes in the near future).

- The form submit button is contained inside its own **fieldset** with **class="submit."** You'll frequently have multiple actions at the end of a form, such as "submit" and "cancel." In such instances, it's quite handy to be able to group these actions, and a **fieldset** does this perfectly. If any styles are applied to normal **fieldset** elements, you'll most often want to have a different style for the **fieldset** surrounding these actions, so the class is necessary to distinguish our actions **fieldset**. The **fieldset** and the input inside it both have the same class name because the term "submit" makes sense for both of them, but it's easy to distinguish them in the CSS by preceding the class selector with an element selector, as we'll see below.

Applying General Form Styling

There are a number of styles which we'll apply to our forms, irrespective of which layout we choose. These styles revolve mainly around the inclusion of whitespace to help separate form elements and **fieldset** elements:

```
fieldset {
  margin: 1.5em 0 0 0;
  padding: 0;
}
legend {
  margin-left: 1em;
  color: #000000;
  font-weight: bold;
}
fieldset ol {
  padding: 1em 1em 0 1em;
  list-style: none;
}
fieldset li {
  padding-bottom: 1em;
}
fieldset.submit {
  border-style: none;
}
```

The **margin** on the **fieldset** helps to separate each **fieldset** group from the others. All internal **padding** is removed from the **fieldset** now, because later on it'll cause problems when we begin floating elements and giving them a **width**. Since **padding** isn't included in the **width**, it can break the dimensions of your form if you have a **width** of **100%** and some **padding**. Removing **padding** also helps to sort out inconsistencies between browsers as to the default internal spacing on the **fieldset**.

To help define a visual hierarchy that clearly shows each **label** inside the **fieldset** grouped under the **legend**, we give our **legend** elements a **font-weight** of **bold**. We also have to replace the spacing that was removed from the **padding** on the **fieldset**, so we give the **legend** a **margin-left** of **1em**.

In order to turn off the natural numbering that would appear for the ordered list, we set **list-style** to **none** on the **ol**, and thus remove any of the bullet formatting that normally exists in such a list. Then, to recreate the internal spacing which we removed from the **fieldset**, we give the ordered list some **padding**. No **padding** is put on the bottom of the list, because this will be taken up by the **padding** of the last list item.

To separate each form element/label pair from each other pair, we give the containing list item a **padding-bottom** of **1em**.

Finally, to remove the appearance of the submit button as a form element group, we need to take the borders off its surrounding `fieldset`. This step is achieved by targeting it using the `fieldset.submit` selector and setting the `border-style` to `none`.

After applying all of this markup and adding some general page layout styles, we end up with Figure 5.8—a form that's beginning to take shape, but is still a bit messy.

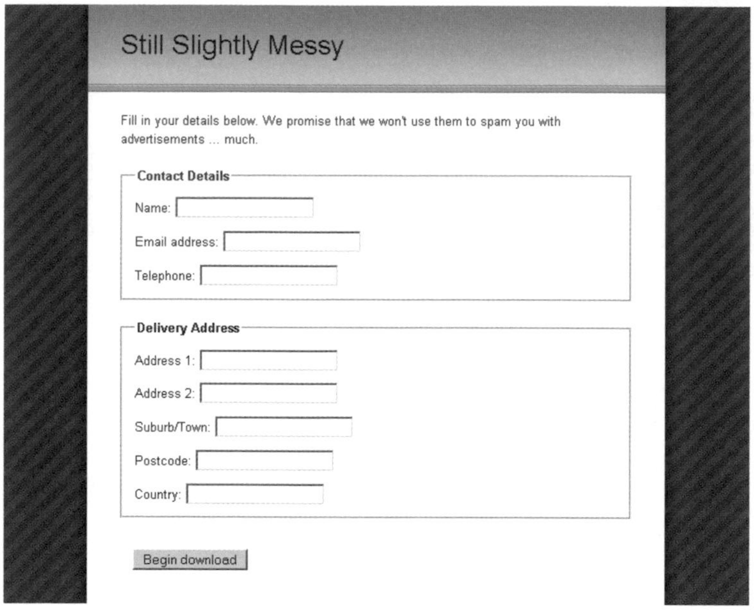

Figure 5.8: Form with general styling applied, but no layout styles

Now we can go ahead and add in some layout styles!

Using Top-positioned Text Labels

Positioning labels at the top of their form elements is probably the easiest layout to achieve, as we only need to tell the `label` to take up the entire width of its parent element.

As our form elements/labels are inside ordered list items (which are block elements), each pair will naturally fall onto a new line, as you can see from Figure 5.9. All we have to do is get the form elements and labels onto different lines.

This exercise is easily completed by turning the `label` elements into block elements, so that they'll occupy an entire line:

```
label {
  display: block;
}
```

It's a simple change, but one which makes the form much neater, as shown in Figure 5.9.

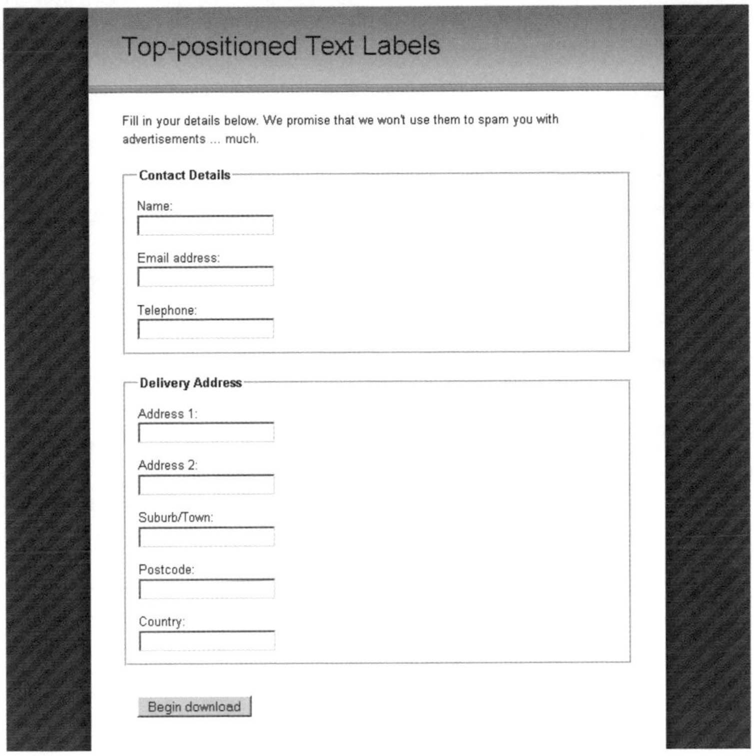

Figure 5.9: Example form with text labels positioned at the top of each form element

Left-aligning Text Labels

When we create a column of text labels to the left of the form elements, we'll have to do a little bit more work than just to position them at the top. Once we begin floating elements, all hell breaks loose!

In order to position the labels next to the form elements, we **float** the **label** elements to the left and give them an explicit **width**:

```
label {
  float: left;
  width: 10em;
  margin-right: 1em;
}
```

We also apply a little bit of **margin-right** to each **label**, so that the text of the **label** can never push right up next to the form element. We must define an explicit **width** on the floated element so that all the form elements will line up in a neat vertical column. The exact width we apply will depend upon the length of the form labels. If possible, the longest form label should be accommodated without wrapping, but there shouldn't be such a large gap that the smallest label looks like it's unconnected to its form element. In the latter scenario, it is okay to have a **label width** that is smaller than the longest **label**, because the text will wrap naturally anyway, as you can see in Figure 5.10.

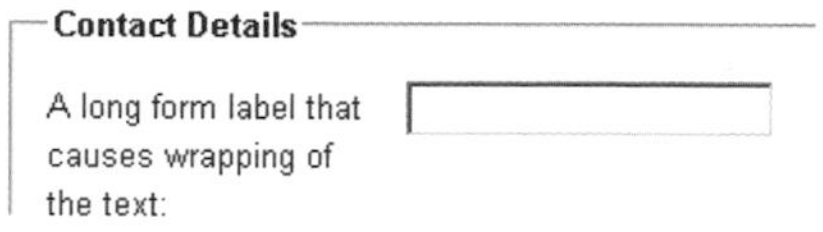

Figure 5.10: Text in floated **label** wraps automatically

Once we float the **label**, however, we run into a problem with its containing list item—the list item will not expand to match the height of the floated element. This problem is highly visible in Figure 5.11, where we've applied a **background-color** to the list item.

Figure 5.11: **li** containing floated **label** does not expand to match **label** height

One markup-free solution to ensuring a parent contains any of its floated children is to also float the parent, so that's what we'll do:

```
                                           left-aligned-labels.css (excerpt)

fieldset li {
  float: left;
  clear: left;
  width: 100%;
  padding-bottom: 1em;
}
```

If the list item is floated, it'll contain all of its floated children, but its **width** must then be set to **100%**, because floated elements try to contract to the smallest width possible. Setting the **width** of the list item to **100%** means that it'll still behave as if it were an unfloated block element. We also throw a **clear :left** property declaration in there to make sure that we won't find any unwanted floating of list items around **form** elements. **clear: left** means that the list item will always appear beneath any prior left-floated elements instead of beside them.

However, once we float the list item, we find the same unwanted behavior on the **fieldset**— it won't expand to encompass the floated list items. So, we have to float the **fieldset**. This is the main reason that we removed the `padding` from `fieldset` earlier—when we set its `width` to `100%`, any `padding` will throw out our dimensions:

left-aligned-labels.css (excerpt)

```
fieldset {
  float: left;
  clear: left;
  width: 100%;
  margin: 0 0 1.5em 0;
  padding: 0;
}
```

Where will this float madness end? Remain calm. It ends right here, with the submit `fieldset`. Since it's the last `fieldset` in the form, and because it doesn't need as much special CSS styling as the other `fieldset`s, we can turn off that floating behavior for good:

left-aligned-labels.css (excerpt)

```
fieldset.submit {
  float: none;
  width: auto;
  border: 0 none #FFF;
  padding-left: 12em;
}
```

By turning off floating and setting the `width` back to `auto`, the final submit `fieldset` becomes a normal block element that clears all the other floats. This means the form will grow to encompass all the `fieldset` elements, and we're back in the normal flow of the document.

None of the elements in the submit `fieldset` are floated, but we want the button to line up with all of the other form elements. To achieve this outcome, we apply `padding` to the actual `fieldset` itself, and this action pushes the submit button across to line up with all the text fields. It's best to have the button line up with the form elements, because it forms a direct linear path that the user's eye can follow when he or she is completing the form.

After all that floating, we now have Figure 5.12—a form with a column for the form labels and a column for the form elements.

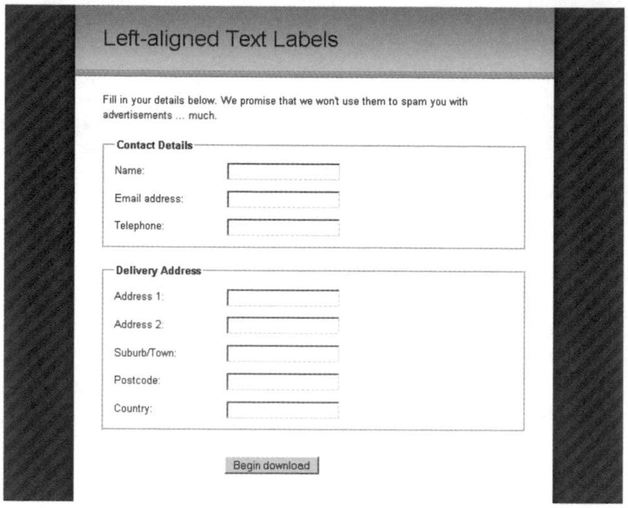

Figure 5.12: Example form with **label** elements organized in left-aligned column

Right-aligning Text Labels

With all that difficult floating safely out of the way, aligning the **input** labels to the right is a breeze; simply set the text alignment on the **label** elements to achieve a form that looks like Figure 5.13:

right-aligned-labels.css (excerpt)

```
label {
  float: left;
  width: 10em;
  margin-right: 1em;
  text-align: right;
}
```

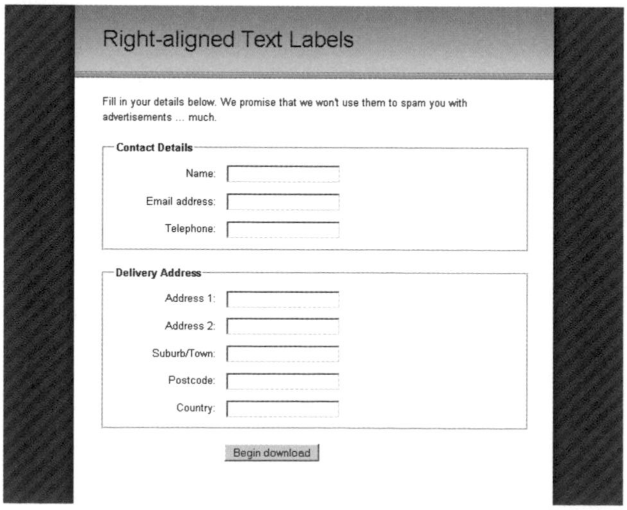

Figure 5.13: Example form with **label** elements organized in right-aligned column

And we're done! Now you can take your pick of whichever form layout best fits your pages, all by changing a little CSS!

Applying `fieldset` and `legend` Styles

It's actually fairly rare to see a `fieldset` displayed in the default browser style. For some reason people just don't like the look of them, and I must admit those borders and `legend` elements don't fit into a lot of page designs. `legend` elements are one of the trickiest HTML elements to style, but you can use a number of tricks to tame them, and there are some great ways to differentiate `fieldset` elements using CSS.

Providing a background color for your `fieldset` elements helps to differentiate `form` content from normal content and focuses the user's attention on the `form` fields themselves. However, it's not as simple as just specifying a `background-color`.

Resolving Internet Explorer's Legends Issues

In a totally unexpected turn of events (yeah, right!) Internet Explorer handles legends differently from other browsers. From experimentation, it seems that Internet Explorer treats `legend` elements as if they're *inside* the `fieldset`, while other browsers treat them as if they're *outside* the `fieldset`. I'm not saying that any browser's wrong, but we have to circumvent these differences somehow, and creating a separate IE style sheet seems to be the best solution.

If you put a `background-color` on a `fieldset` with a `legend`, as in Figure 5.14, you can see the problem all too clearly.

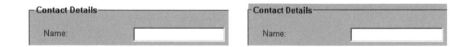

Figure 5.14: Browser rendering of **fieldset** elements with background color

The `fieldset` on the left shows how most browsers render a `legend` and `fieldset` with a background color. The `fieldset` on the right shows how Internet Explorer renders it—the `background-color` of the `fieldset` appears to extend beyond its border, stretching to fit the height of the `legend`.

The way to avoid this problem is to accomodate Internet Explorer browsers with a separate style sheet that uses conditional comments:

```
<!--[if lte IE 7]>
  <style type="text/css" media="all">
    @import "css/fieldset-styling-ie.css";
  </style>
<![endif]-->
```

This statement includes a style sheet for Internet Explorer 7 and earlier, as these are the versions that currently display this deviant behavior. Any other browsers will ignore it. We could use a style sheet that applies to any version of Internet Explorer—including those released in the future—but the **legend** display difference may be corrected by then, so it's safest just to apply it to the versions we know for the present.

Inside that style sheet we use relative positioning on the **legend** to move it up to align with the top of the **fieldset**:

```
legend {
  position: relative;
  left: -7px;
  top: -0.75em;
}
fieldset ol {
  padding-top: 0.25em;
}
```

In this case, the value we've given the **legend**'s **top**—**0.75em**—just happens to be the right value to get the **legend** to align with the **fieldset**. It may vary depending on other styles we might apply to the legend (such as margin and padding). This is quite a robust solution— we've used relative units, so if users change the text size in their browsers, the position of the **legend** will shift accordingly and still line up.

In addition to moving the top of the **legend**, we move it 7px to the left by applying a **left** value of **-7px**. This step counters an Internet Explorer quirk—IE always shifts legends to the right by 7px (regardless of text size), so we need to negate that shift to get the **legend** and the **label** elements lining up neatly.

Because we're moving the legend up relatively, it will create more space below the **legend**. To counteract this space, we reduce the padding at the top of the ordered list by an equivalent amount, changing it from the original value of **1em** to **0.25em**.

The last Internet Explorer fix is to relatively position the **fieldset** itself:

```
fieldset {
  position: relative;
}
```

Without this rule, Internet Explorer produces some weird visual effects around the **legend**. How weird? You can see exactly how weird in Figure 5.15.

Figure 5.15: Visual aberrations in Internet Explorer

We really need to avoid the IE aberrations we've seen, but we're almost there—now we'll just set the **position** of the **fieldset** to **relative** to restore everything to normal.

Styling Legends and Fieldsets

In all browsers, **legend**s will have some **padding** by default. The amount of **padding** varies between browsers, so to have the **legend** lining up nicely with our **label**s we'll eliminate the **padding** in our main style sheet:

```
                                            fieldset-background-color.css (excerpt)

legend {
  margin-left: 1em;
  padding: 0;
  color: #000;
  font-weight: bold;
}
```

The default **border** for **fieldset** elements is normally an inset border—which doesn't match some sites—so here we're going to make it a flat, 1px border. In addition, we'll add in a background color that will make the **fieldset** elements stand out from the normal page background, marking them as special areas:

```
                                            fieldset-background-color.css (excerpt)

fieldset {
  float: left;
  clear: both;
  width: 100%;
  margin: 0 0 1.5em 0;
  padding: 0;
  border: 1px solid #BFBAB0;
  background-color: #F2EFE9;
}
```

Generally speaking, we don't want any borders or background color behind the submit **fieldset**, so it's quite easy to turn those off:

```
                                           fieldset-background-color.css (excerpt)
fieldset.submit {
  float: none;
  width: auto;
  border-style: none;
  padding-left: 12em;
  background-color: transparent;
}
```

Now we've got **fieldset** elements with a background color and a **legend** that lines up neatly with all the other form elements, as in Figure 5.16.

Figure 5.16: **fieldset** elements with **background-color** set and adjustments made to **legend**

The cut-off of color behind the **legend** can sometimes look a bit abrupt, as you can see in the magnified view of the **legend** shown in Figure 5.17.

Figure 5.17: Magnification of **legend**—cut-off of background color is apparent

This cut-off will become more pronounced if we use a **fieldset** background color that has more contrast with the normal page background color. If you want to counteract this effect, it's possible to put a gradient background image into the **fieldset** that smoothly changes the color from the page background color (white) to your chosen **fieldset** background color:

fieldset-background-image.css (excerpt)

```
fieldset {
  float: left;
  clear: both;
  width: 100%;
  margin: 0 0 1.5em 0;
  padding: 0;
  border: 1px solid #BFBAB0;
  background-color: #F2EFE9;
  background-image: url(images/fieldset_gradient.jpg);
  background-repeat: repeat-x;
}
```

That `background-image` rule will also be applied to our submit `fieldset`, so to keep a clean, transparent background, we'll also have to cancel the `background-image` on the submit `fieldset`:

fieldset-background-image.css (excerpt)

```
fieldset.submit {
  float: none;
  width: auto;
  border-style: none;
  padding-left: 12em;
  background-color: transparent;
  background-image: none;
}
```

See Figure 5.18—the form looks a lot smoother, no?

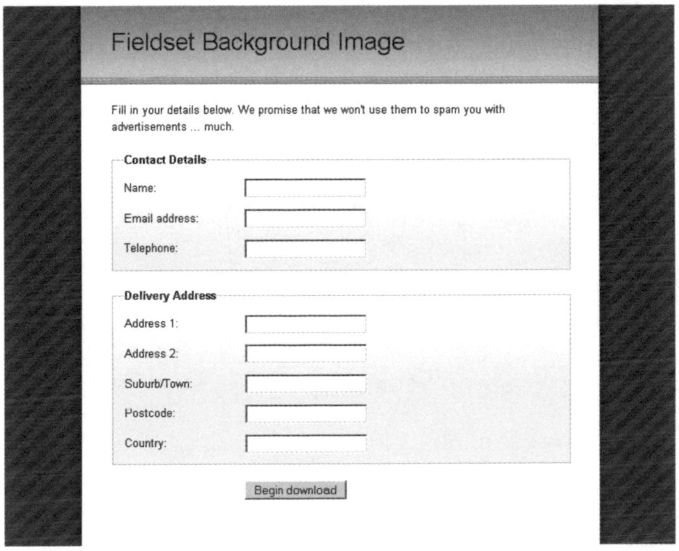

Figure 5.18: **fieldset** elements with background color and gradient images applied

Changing the Default Fieldset Layout

Although **fieldset** and **legend** elements are the most accessible means of marking up form groups, in the past a lot of people haven't used them because they don't like the default styling that browsers impose on these elements—the border around the **fieldset**, the **legend** intersecting the edge of the box. But it *is* possible to change this default layout and make your forms a little less boxy.

Our first step is to push the **fieldset** elements together, eliminating the whitespace between them. To do this, we could make the **margin** on the bottom of the **fieldset** elements zero, but that actually ends up looking like Figure 5.19.

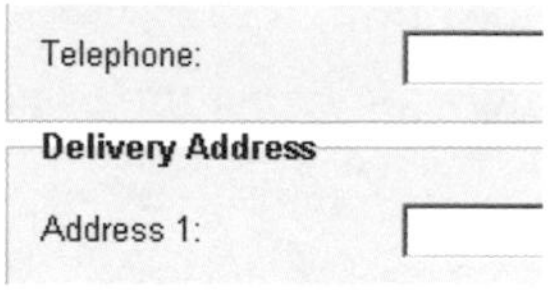

Figure 5.19: **legend** adding extra height so **fieldset** elements cannot touch

The **legend** at the top of the **fieldset** elements prevents the two **fieldset** elements from joining.To circumvent this problem we can use some negative **margin** on the bottom of each **fieldset**. This will "pull" up the lower **fieldset** so that it overlaps the upper **fieldset**, making it look like they're touching.

To prevent the bottom **fieldset** from overlapping any form elements, we should also add a bit of padding to the bottom of the **fieldset** elements so that they've got some space to move into:

```
fieldset {
  float: left;
  clear: both;
  width: 100%;
  margin: 0 0 -1em 0;
  padding: 0 0 1em 0;
  border: 1px solid #BFBAB0;
  background-color: #F2EFE9;
}
```

Moving the **fieldset**s up by **1em** is enough to cover the gap between them, and the **bottom-padding** of **1em** counteracts the movement, making sure no **form** elements disappear beneath **fieldset** elements.

A couple of visual tweaks are necessary when removing the whitespace. Without contact between the **fieldset** background color and the normal page background color, we no longer need the gradient background image, so this has been left out.

The **border-style** has also been changed—we're removing all borders, then replacing only the top border:

```
fieldset {
  float: left;
  clear: both;
  width: 100%;
  margin: 0 0 -1em 0;
  padding: 0 0 1em 0;
  border-style: none;
  border-top: 1px solid #BFBAB0;
  background-color: #F2EFE9;
}
```

With all the **fieldset** elements being joined together, the extra borders on the left and right make the form look cluttered. With just a top border, we've created a much cleaner look, as shown in Figure 5.20.

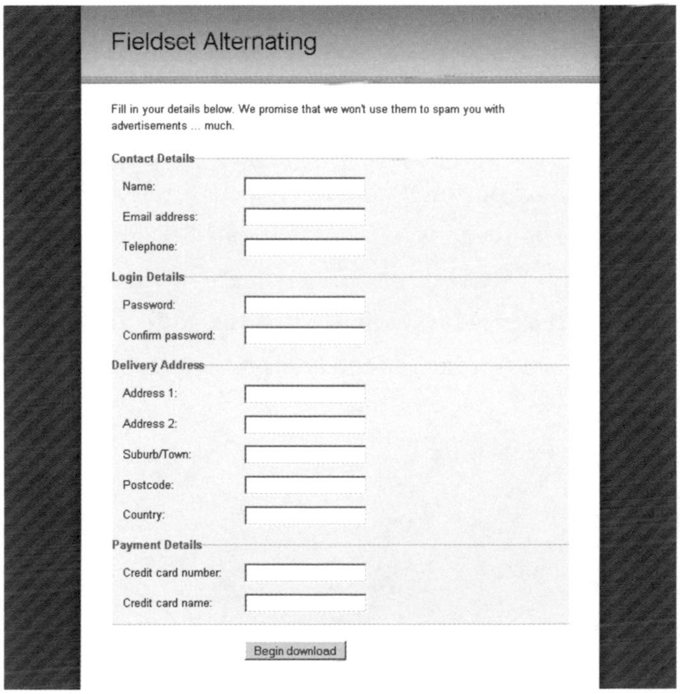

Figure 5.20: Joined **fieldset** elements

The other side effect of joining the **fieldset** elements together is that the **legend** now looks out of place, balancing in between either **fieldset**. The way to solve this problem is to bring the **legend** fully within the boundaries of its **fieldset**.

Instinctively, you might use relative or absolute positioning on the `legend` to move it down into the `fieldset`. However, Firefox resists any attempt to reposition the `legend`—it just doesn't move.

Unfortunately, the only way around this issue is to add a tiny bit more markup to our form. By inserting a superfluous `span` into each of our `legend` elements, Firefox allows us to style this and move the text down into the `fieldset`:

fieldset-alternating.html (excerpt)

```
<legend>
  <span>Contact Details</span>
</legend>
```

That `span` can be positioned absolutely and moved down into the `fieldset` using `margin-top`. While we're at it, let's also increase the `font-size` of the `legend` text, to give it a bit more prominence:

fieldset-alternating.css (excerpt)

```
legend span {
  position: absolute;
  margin-top: 0.5em;
  font-size: 135%;
}
```

There's actually an esoteric bug in some point releases of Firefox (Firefox 1.5.0.6 on Windows XP, but not OSX, from what I've seen) that makes the absolutely positioned `span` elements behave as if they were all positioned at the top of the form element. Giving the `legend` elements a `position` of `relative` doesn't seem to affect the `span` elements, so we actually need to relatively position each of the `fieldset` elements and give the `span` elements some explicit coordinates to sidestep this bug:

fieldset-alternating.css (excerpt)

```
fieldset {
  position: relative;
  float: left;
  clear: both;
  width: 100%;
  margin: 0 0 -1em 0;
  padding: 0 0 1em 0;
  border-style: none;
  border-top: 1px solid #BFBAB0;
  background-color: #F2EFE9;
}
```

```
legend span {
  position: absolute;
  left: 0.74em;
  top: 0;
  margin-top: 0.5em;
  font-size: 135%;
}
```

The **0.74em** value of **left** actually matches the **1em padding** we gave to the ordered list, due to the fact that the **span** has a larger **font-size**.

Because we're now specifying a **left** ordinate for the **span**, we also have to take the **margin-left** off its parent **legend**, so that we don't get a doubling of the spacing. Simply omit the **margin** rule that we used previously:

fieldset-alternating.css (excerpt)

```
legend {
  padding: 0;
  color: #545351;
  font-weight: bold;
}
```

That bug's now squashed!

As we're moving the **legend** down into the **fieldset**, we need to make sure that the **legend** won't overlap any of the form elements, so let's add a bit more **padding** to the top of our ordered list:

fieldset-alternating.css (excerpt)

```
fieldset ol {
  padding: 3.5em 1em 0 1em;
  list-style: none;
}
```

Don't forget to change the matching value inside our Internet Explorer-only style sheet:

fieldset-alternating-ie.css (excerpt)

```
legend span {
  margin-top: 1.25em;
}
fieldset ol {
  padding-top: 3.25em;
}
```

Internet Explorer has slightly different spacing on the **legend** element's **span**, so let's tweak the **margin-top** value for that as well.

After all these changes, there's one **fieldset** that looks a little out-of-place: the submit **fieldset**. Because the submit **fieldset** doesn't have a **legend**, the submit button will be moved up too high, so we need to push it down a bit. This is done most easily by adding some **padding** to the top of this **fieldset** only. Also, because the submit **fieldset** will overlap the **fieldset** above it, we need to provide a solid **background-color** for the submit **fieldset**, otherwise the previous **fieldset**'s **background-color** will shrow through. This means changing the **background-color** value from **transparent** to whatever your normal page **background-color** is:

fieldset-alternating.css (excerpt)

```
fieldset.submit {
  float: none;
  width: auto;
  padding-top: 1.5em;
  padding-left: 12em;
  background-color: #FFFFFF;
}
```

Figure 5.21: All **fieldset** elements joined and **legend** elements moved inside boxes

Previously, we also removed borders from the submit **fieldset**, but for this adjoining layout we need the submit **fieldset** to retain the top border that's applied to all **fieldset** elements. We'll just let that rule cascade into the submit **fieldset** without interference.

Once we've implemented all those changes, the layout of the form is complete. The form appears as shown in Figure 5.21, but it requires some slight aesthetic tweaks.

Because we've pushed all the **fieldset** elements together, they tend to run into one another visually. Better distinction can be created between each **fieldset** by subtle alternation of the **background-color** elements in odd and even **fieldset** elements. The only cross-browser method for achieving this is to add in a new class for every second **fieldset**. This allows us to use a CSS selector to give those **fieldset** elements a different **background-color**. I normally use a **class** of **alt**, but you can use whatever you think is logical:

```
<fieldset>
…
</fieldset>
<fieldset class="alt">
…
</fieldset>
<fieldset>
…
</fieldset>
<fieldset class="alt">
…
</fieldset>
…
```

Then all you have to do is think of a different **background-color**:

fieldset-alternating.css (excerpt)

```
fieldset.alt {
  background-color: #E6E3DD;
}
```

And our final **form** with alternating **fieldset** elements looks like Figure 5.22!

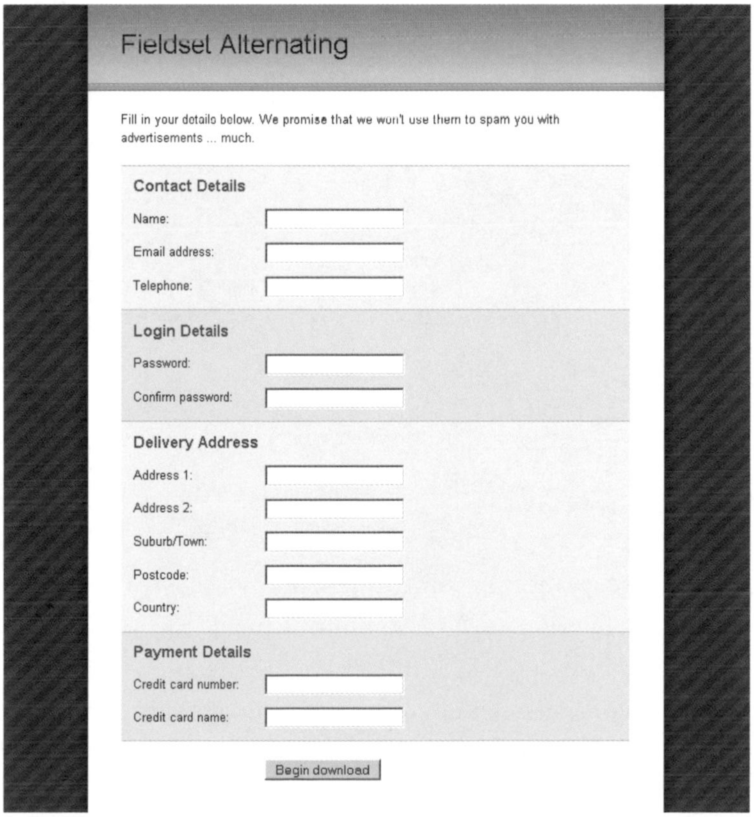

Grouping Radio Buttons and Checkboxes

There are two types of form elements that are likely to be part of their own subgroup. These are checkboxes and radio buttons, both of which can be used to offer users multiple choices when responding to a given question on a form.

Figure 5.22: Alternating-color **fieldset** elements

The way in which these form elements are laid out is slightly different to text fields, `select` boxes or `textareas`. As they are part of their own subgroup, they should be included in a nested `fieldset` inside the main `fieldset`. Using our `background-image form` as a starting point, we can add some grouped elements inside the `fieldset`:

element-subgroups.html (excerpt)

```
<fieldset>
  <legend>Contact Details</legend>
  <ol>
    <li>
      <fieldset>
        <legend>Occupation:</legend>
        <ol>
          <li>
            <input id="occupation1" name="occupation1"
                class="checkbox" type="checkbox" value="1" />
            <label for="occupation1">Doctor</label>
          </li>
          <li>
            <input id="occupation2" name="occupation2"
                class="checkbox" type="checkbox" value="1" />
            <label for="occupation2">Lawyer</label>
          </li>
          <li>
            <input id="occupation3" name="occupation3"element
                class="checkbox" type="checkbox" value="1" />
            <label for="occupation3">Teacher</label>
          </li>
          <li>
            <input id="occupation4" name="occupation4"
                class="checkbox" type="checkbox" value="1" />
            <label for="occupation4">Web designer</label>
          </li>
        </ol>
      </fieldset>
    </li>
  </ol>
</fieldset>
```

The `label` for the subgroup actually becomes the `legend` for the nested `fieldset`, then each of the checkboxes or radio buttons inside the `fieldset` receives its own `label`. The ordered list structure that was put in place at the top level is replicated on this sub-level as well, more for consistency than necessity although it can be very handy if you want to style some of the sub-items.

The nested elements will inherit the styles that we put in place for top-level items, so we'll have to set some rules specifically for nested elements before they'll display correctly:

element-subgroups.css (excerpt)

```
fieldset fieldset {
  margin-bottom: -2.5em;
  border-style: none;
  background-color: transparent;
  background-image: none;
}
fieldset fieldset legend {
  margin-left: 0;
  font-weight: normal;
}
fieldset fieldset ol {
  position: relative;
  top: -1.5em;
  margin: 0 0 0 11em;
  padding: 0;
}
fieldset fieldset label {
  float: none;
  width: auto;
  margin-right: auto;
}
```

Firstly, all the decoration on the nested **fieldset** is removed: **background-color**, **background-image**, and **border** properties. Instead, it's given a negative **margin-bottom** for the purposes of some trickery we'll see in a moment.

We want to make the **legend** look exactly like a normal **label**, so we remove the left margin and also take off its bold **font-weight**. It's important to be careful with the length of text inside the **legend**, as most browsers won't wrap the text in a **legend**. As a result, any **width** you've set for the legend/text will be ignored, as the text will just continue on in one line, possibly running over the rest of the **form**. We can overcome this limitation by exercising a maximum character width for the **legend** text and sizing the **form** columns in **em** units, so that with text-resizing the layout will scale accordingly.

> **NOTE   Limitations of legend**
>
> Along with the inability of **legend** elements to wrap text, they are also resistant to **width** settings and text alignment. This use of **legend** elements for grouping within **fieldset** elements is only possible for left-aligned **label** elements, not right-aligned **label** elements.

We use the ordered list to position the nested form elements and **label** elements. Its left **margin** pushes the entire container away from the left edge, equivalent to the amount of **margin** given to form elements at the top level. Then, to bring the top of the form elements in line with the top of their respective **legend**, we need to position the ordered list relatively and move it up by **-1.5em**. This will leave a large space at the bottom of the list (where the list would have been if it wasn't moved relatively), and this is where the **fieldset**'s negative **margin** comes into play. The negative **margin** pulls up the content after the **fieldset** by the same amount we moved the ordered list, making it look like there is no empty gap. The **padding** that's put on ordered lists at the top level isn't needed here, so we just set this property to **0**.

The last thing we need to do is to revert our **label** elements to their native state. This means we stop them from floating and set their **width** to **auto**. Because they're inline elements, they'll now sit nicely next to the actual form elements—checkboxes or radio buttons.

There's an additional change to make to the Internet Explorer-specific style sheet: to turn off the negative relative position on nested **legend**s. We don't have to deal with background colors on the nested **fieldset** elements, so the negative relative position isn't needed here:

element-subgroups-ie.css (excerpt)

```
fieldset fieldset legend {
  top: 0;
}
```

Once those new styles have been created, we end up with the form that appears in Figure 5.23—a nested **fieldset** that lines up perfectly with all the other form elements and gives the user a nice straightforward choice of options.

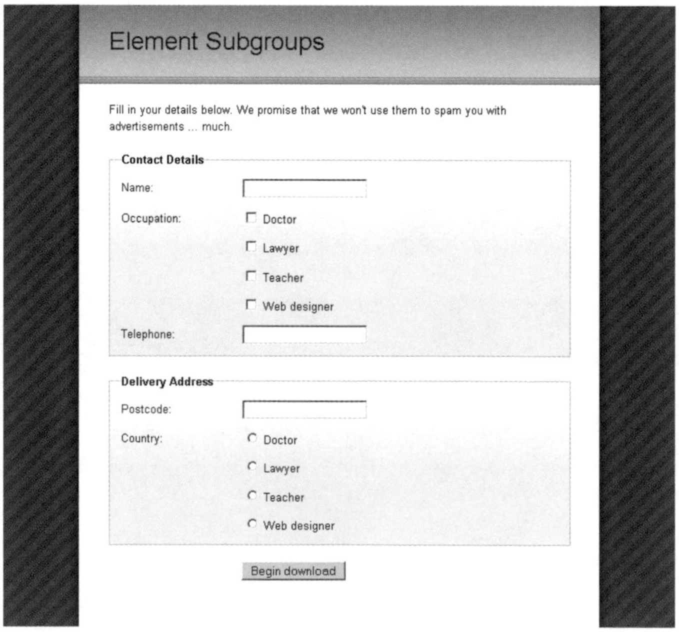

Figure 5.23: Nested subgroups of checkboxes and radio buttons

Required Fields and Error Messages

There are often little extra bits of information that you want to convey on a form, and they should be equally as accessible as the text **label** elements for the form element. In fact, to ensure that they're accessible, they should be included in the **label** itself. There are two types that we'll look at here: required fields and error messages.

Indicating Required Fields

The easiest and most accessible way of indicating the required fields on a form is to write "required" after the form **label**. This addition is not only read out by screenreaders, but it also means that an extra symbol key doesn't need to be provided for visual users, as is the case should you choose to mark required fields with an asterisk or other symbol.

To emphasize the importance of the information, we can add the text "required" inside an **em** element, which also gives us a stylable element to differentiate the "required" text from the **label** text:

required-fields.html (excerpt)

```
<label for="name">
  Name: <em>required</em>
</label>
```

To give the **em** its own little place on the **form**, we can set it to **display: block**, and change the appearance of the text:

required-fields.css (excerpt)

```
label em {
  display: block;
  color: #060;
  font-size: 85%;
  font-style: normal;
  text-transform: uppercase;
}
```

Our "required" markers now look like this:

Figure 5.24: Form fields marked with textual "required" markers

However, the asterisk, or star, has now become a common tool for marking required fields, possibly due to its brevity. But it doesn't have much meaning outside the visual context—most screenreaders will read an asterisk character as "star." So you end up with a `label` being "Email address star"—a little confusing for the user.

For accessibility purposes, instead of including an actual asterisk character next to the form `label`, it's actually better to include an inline image of the asterisk, with `alt` text saying "required." This means that screenreader users will hear the word "required" instead of just "star," which is a lot more helpful. If you *are* using an image, you should include a key at the top of the `form` to let visual users know exactly what it means.

We still want to emphasize the fact that the `label` is required, so we just replace the text "required" inside the `em` element with the image of an asterisk:

required-fields-star1.html (excerpt)

```
<label for="name">
  Name: <em><img src="images/required_star.gif"
    alt="required" /></em>
</label>
```

This replacement doesn't actually need any styling; we can leave the `em` as an inline element and the asterisk will appear directly next to the form `label`:

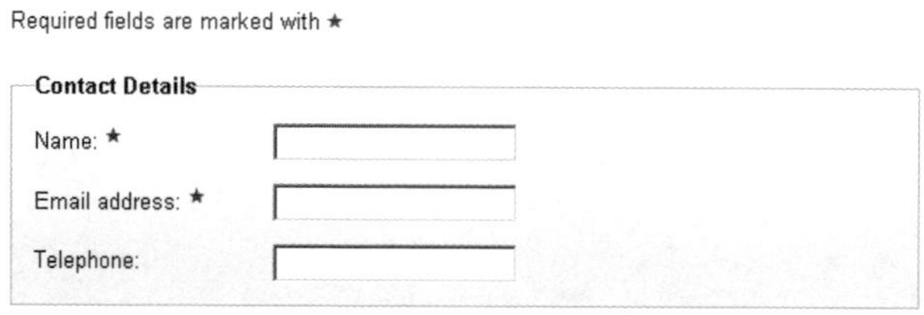

Figure 5.25: Inline asterisk marking required fields

Or, we can use some CSS to position the image absolutely and have it more closely associated with the form element itself:

required-fields-star2.css (excerpt)

```
label {
  position: relative;
  float: left;
  width: 10em;
  margin-right: 1em;
}
```

```
label em {
  position: absolute;
  left: 10em;
  top: 0;
}
```

When positioning the **em** absolutely, it's important to position its parent (the **label**) relatively, so that when we specify some coordinates for the **em**, they will be relative to the **label**'s top-left corner. The star image should be positioned in the gap between the **label** and the form element (created by the **label**'s right **margin**), so the value for the **em**'s **left** will depend upon what we've set there. Setting the top value for the **em** is just a precaution in case the image has wrapped onto a new line.

By taking this course of action, we'll end up with a much more orderly series of "required" markers, as shown in Figure 5.26.

Figure 5.26: Required fields marked with absolutely positioned image of a star, aligned against form elements

Handling Error Messages

Error messages are handled in almost the same way as required markers. In order to be read out as a screenreader user places focus on the appropriate form element, they should form part of the **label**:

error-fields1.html (excerpt)

```
<label for="name">
  Email: <strong>This must be a valid email address</strong>
</label>
```

The semantic **strong** element is used to enclose the error message, distinguishing it from a required marker and giving it a stronger emphasis.

The styling is almost the same as it was for the textual "required" marker, except you might want to change the color. A good strong red is suitably alarming:

```
                                           error-fields1.css (excerpt)
label strong {
  display: block;
  color: #C00;
  font-size: 85%;
  font-weight: normal;
  text-transform: uppercase;
}
```

This styling produces a layout such as that shown in Figure 5.27.

Figure 5.27: Error messages included as part of **label** element, displayed underneath the **label** text

An alternative placement of the error message does exist, but it depends upon a couple of prerequisites. The error message can be placed to the right of the form element as long as:

- The maximum width of any of the **form** elements is known.
- The error message is unlikely to wrap.

This placement involves the error message being positioned absolutely, so we must know in advance how far to move the error. Absolute elements are outside the flow of the document, so the other content will not adjust to accommodate the error message if it starts wrapping. If the design can be reconciled with these two problems, then the CSS for the job is:

```
                                           error-fields2.css (excerpt)
label {
  position: relative;
  float: left;
  width: 10em;
  margin-right: 1em;
}
```

```
label strong {
  position: absolute;
  left: 27em;
  top: 0.2em;
  width: 19em;
  color: #C00;
  font-size: 85%;
  font-weight: normal;
  text-transform: uppercase;
}
```

Again, because the **strong** element is being positioned absolutely, its parent **label** must be positioned relatively to allow us to move the error message relative to the **label** itself.

The **width** of the error message is dictated by the space following the form element. The **left** is calculated by adding together the **width** of the form element, plus the **width** of the **label**, plus any extra space we need in order to align the error message properly.

Figure 5.28 shows how it ends up when viewed in the browser.

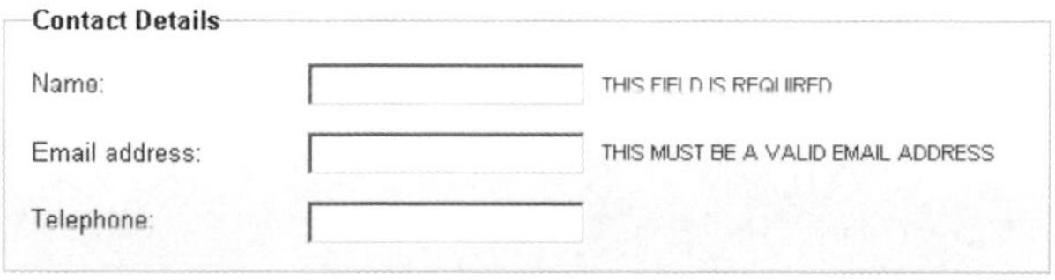

Figure 5.28: Error messages as part of the **label** element, displayed using absolute positioning

NOTE *Inaccessible Error Text Solutions*

It is possible to position the error text to the right of the text fields by changing the source order of the HTML. But this either:

- places the error text outside the **label**
- involves nesting the **form** element inside the **label** and placing the error text after the form element

Both of these solutions are inaccessible because screenreaders will most likely fail to read out the error message when the **form** element is focused.

In conjunction with right-positioning the error messages, we can also include error icons, to further highlight the problem areas on the form. The error icon is included in the HTML with an appropriate **alt** attribute:

error-fields3.html (excerpt)

```
<fieldset>
  <legend>Contact Details</legend>
  <ol>
    <li>
      <label for="name">
        Email: <strong><img src="images/error_cross.gif"
          alt="Error" /> This must be a valid email address
          </strong>
      </label>
      <input id="name" name="name" class="text" type="text" />
    </li>
```

We can now move it to the left of the form elements using absolute positioning. Because its parent (the **strong** element) is already absolutely positioned, any movement we make will be relative to that parent, so, effectively, we have to move it in a negative direction in order to shift it back over to the left:

error-fields3.css (excerpt)

```
label strong img {
  position: absolute;
  left: -16em;
}
```

This adjustment equates to the width of the form element, plus a little bit extra for spacing, so we'll get a nicely positioned icon, such as you can see in Figure 5.29.

Figure 5.29: Error messages displaying to right of **form** elements, in combination with error icon on left

Summary

Now that you've finished this chapter, you have no excuse for producing inaccessible forms that use tables for positioning!

We've worked through the correct and effective labeling, grouping, layout, and styling of form elements, anticipating and solving potential problems of compatibility and accessibility along the way. With the code provided here you've got quite a few different options for how you want your forms laid out, but there's still more you can do by combining and experimenting with different styles, form elements and layouts.

If there's an underlying message of this chapter, it's just to keep in mind that no matter what you do, your forms have to be usable and accessible above everything else. Forms, at the end of the day, are really all about your users being able to provide information and tell you what they want as easily as possible.

Rounded Corners

Serving Sushi

More traditionally, sushi is served on minimalist Japanese-style, geometric, wood or lacquer plates which are mono- or duo-tone in color, in keeping with the aesthetic qualities of this cuisine.

Many small sushi restaurants actually use no plates — the sushi is eaten directly off of the wooden counter, usually with one's hands, despite the historical tradition of eating nigiri with chopsticks.

Ever since Tim Berners-Lee prototyped HTML elements as rectangular boxes of content back in 1992, designers have been trying to elude those corners. Boxes with rounded corners are a commonly used design element—one that *should* be easily achieved in HTML with the help of CSS. This is most noticeably true with the CSS 3 `background` properties, which grant us the ability to apply multiple backgrounds to a single element. It's this capability that permits us to create the effect of rounded corners on an element.

However, as of this writing, Safari (more specifically, the Webkit rendering engine) is the only mainstream browser to support these advanced properties. To add to this misfortune, given the extent to which today's browsers support CSS 2.1, I'm not counting on seeing the practical benefits of CSS 3 available for quite some time.

 CartographyCorner

That means that we designers must work with what we have. Given the right scenario, adding rounded corners can be a very straightforward process—one that's really all about flexibility. There's one general rule, though: the more flexible the rounded box, the more complicated the markup and CSS. In order to avoid trouble, the careful designer must ask a number of pertinent questions when tackling each step of the process:

- **Determine the required amount of flexibility.**

  Does the box need to stretch vertically? Horizontally? Do I have complete control over the markup? Is the markup going to change?

- **Evaluate the markup.**

  Do I have all the hooks I need? Can I use existing elements? Can I add elements to provide some semantic value?

- **Create the images.**

  Do I need all four corners separately? Can I combine images to reduce the need for additional elements?

- **Apply the styles.**

  Do all my background components line up? Is my padding getting in the way? Does my CSS allow for varying content?

In this chapter, we'll learn to round the corners of both a definition list and a `div` containing a headline and paragraph. Then, we'll put what we've learned into practice to create a web site layout that offers varying levels of flexibility.

Flexibility

We live in the brave new world of The People's Internet—a place where wild assumptions such as "one-size-fits-all" text sizes have been thrown by the wayside, just like that tight denim jacket that *seemed* cool in the '80s. Whether our data is user-generated or stored in a content management system that anyone can use, we can never be certain of the sizing requirements for content containers. Thus, **flexibility** is an essential requirement for any element of your site that will hold content.

Flexibility can be achieved by allowing such elements to resize automatically to fit the content they hold. This resizing may be in the form of **horizontal flexibility** (the width of the container changes), **vertical flexibility** (the height alters), or a combination of both.

Vertical Flexibility

Rounded corners can be accomplished most easily if we only use vertical flexibility, applying a fixed `width` to the container we want to style. The rounded box will extend to fit the content, regardless of whether it's the volume of content or the text size that necessitates the container's increase in height. When the `width` of our item is set in stone, we can use one image for the top two corners, and one for the bottom two, attaching each image to a single element—these requirements are depicted in Figure 6.1.

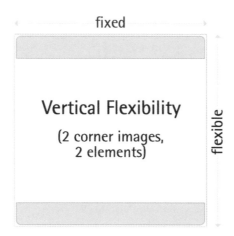

Figure 6.1: Requirements of adding rounded corners to a container with vertical flexibility

Let's begin by rounding the corners of a definition list that contains one title and one definition:

roundabout-feature.html (excerpt)

```
<dl id="feature">
  <dt>Roundabout</dt>
  <dd>A roundabout or rotary is a type of road junction (or
      traffic calming device) at which traffic streams around
      a central island, after first yielding (giving way) to
      the circulating traffic.</dd>
</dl>
```

NOTE *Semantic Identification*

It would be easy to label this element as "rounded" or "roundbox," but this would detract from the semantic nature of our markup. "Rounded" describes presentation, and has no business being in our markup. "Feature" is a much more semantic identification for this element, even though it may seem less descriptive at first glance.

For this first example, let's style our definition list to look like the mockup shown in Figure 6.2.

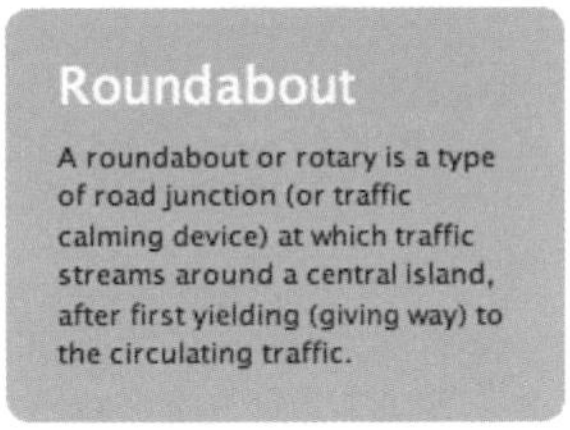

Roundabout

A roundabout or rotary is a type of road junction (or traffic calming device) at which traffic streams around a central island, after first yielding (giving way) to the circulating traffic.

Figure 6.2: Intended design for our fixed-width example

We've set a `width` of 220px on our definition list. The `height` property is left undefined so that it defaults to `auto`, and can adjust to the content as required. The strategy for any rounded-corner box is to put a `background` on the entire box, then cover up the corners with opaque images, which creates the rounded look. From a style sheet and layout perspective, our full-color `background` needs to be on the lowest "layer," or the block-level element that contains the rest of our markup. In our example, this is the `dl` element. Let's see it in CSS:

```
* {
  margin: 0;
  padding: 0;
}
html {
  font: small/1.4 "Lucida Grande", Tahoma, sans-serif;
}
body {
  font-size: 92%;
}
#feature {
  background: #96BF55;
  width: 220px;
}
```

We've added `html` and `body` definitions to style fonts, and we've removed all default `margin`s and `padding` from every element by using the universal selector `*`.[1] As we want our definition term, and definition description, to take up the full `width` of the `dl`, we needn't assign them a `width`, as block-level elements will expand to the full `width` of their containing elements. Figure 6.3 shows what our feature looks like right now.

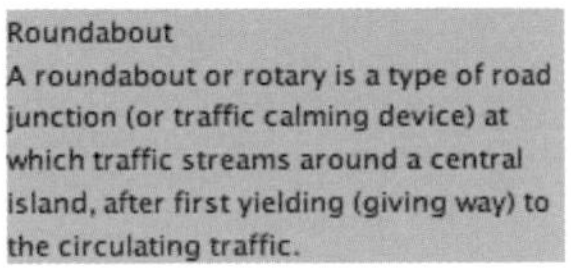

Roundabout
A roundabout or rotary is a type of road junction (or traffic calming device) at which traffic streams around a central island, after first yielding (giving way) to the circulating traffic.

Figure 6.3: Our feature box so far

Before we can put the images in place to cover up the corners of this box, we need to create

1   http://leftjustified.net/journal/2004/10/19/global-ws-reset/

them. The `width` of the box doesn't change, so we only need two images—one to cover the top two corners, and one to cover the bottom two. These images should look like those in Figure 6.4, and be the exact `width` of our element.

Figure 6.4: The two background images we'll need

It's important to note that the white parts in the corners of the image are *not* transparent. They'll need to be colored to match the background behind your rounded box. We'll save these images in a folder called *images*, which will reside in the same directory as our style sheet, and name the files *top.gif* and *bottom.gif*.

To achieve the display shown in Figure 6.5, we need to attach these images as backgrounds to our block-level elements. As background images are placed on top of background colors in CSS, we can put one of these images on the `dl` element where we assigned our `background-color`. We can place the other image on the `dt` like so:

```
#feature {
  background: #96BF55 url(images/bottom.gif) no-repeat bottom left;
  width: 220px;
}
#feature dt {
  background: url(images/top.gif) no-repeat;
  margin: 0;
}
```

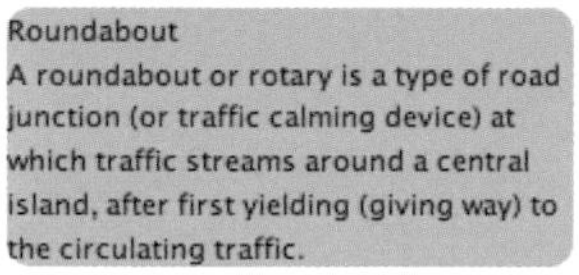

Roundabout
A roundabout or rotary is a type of road junction (or traffic calming device) at which traffic streams around a central island, after first yielding (giving way) to the circulating traffic.

Figure 6.5: Rounded corners completed

Our corners are in place! The `background-position` on the `dt` didn't need to be specified, because we want its background image placed at the top left of the element, which is the default position assumed by the `background` style. The only thing left to do is style our content:

```
#feature {
  background: #96BF55 url(images/bottom.gif) no-repeat bottom
     left;
  width: 220px;
  padding: 0 0 20px;
}
```

```
#feature dt {
  background: url(images/top.gif) no-repeat;
  padding: 20px 20px 0;
  font-size:170%;
  color:#FFF;
  line-height:1;
  margin:0;
}
#feature dd {
  padding: 10px 20px 0;
  color:#1B220F;
  line-height:1.3;
  margin:0;
}
```

NOTE   Unitless Line Height

If you're following our progress closely, you may have noticed that if you try to validate this CSS (at the time of writing), the W3C validator says you can't use unitless integers for **line-height** values, as we do in **#feature dt**. As it turns out, the validator is wrong in this case. If you *really* need to make your CSS validate with the W3C validator, feel free to use **line-height: 1.0** instead—in the validator's infinite wisdom, it mistakes a decimal place for a unit and lets our **line-height** rule slip through.[2]

Here, we're adding some **padding** to each element, increasing the **font-size** of the header, setting the **color**, and modifying **line-height** properties. Let's see our changes in a browser, or even in Figure 6.6.

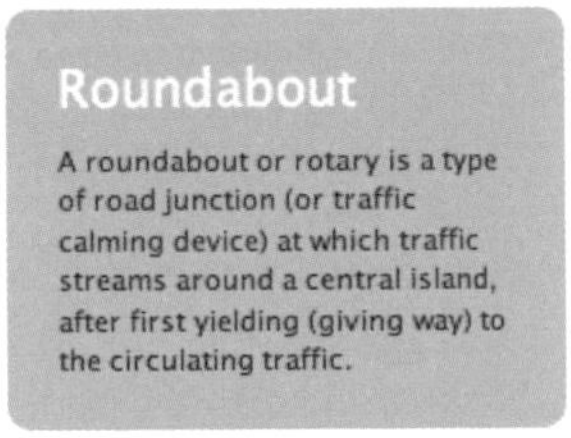

Roundabout

A roundabout or rotary is a type of road junction (or traffic calming device) at which traffic streams around a central island, after first yielding (giving way) to the circulating traffic.

Figure 6.6: The final result

Also, let's see the final version of our style sheet:

```
* {
  margin: 0;
  padding: 0;
}
```

---

2   Check out http://meyerweb.com/eric/thoughts/2006/02/08/unitless-line-heights/ for more on this topic.

```css
html {
  font: small/1.4 "Lucida Grande", Tahoma, sans-serif;
}
body {
  font-size: 92%;
}
#feature {
  background: #96BF55 url(images/bottom.gif) no-repeat bottom left;
  width: 220px;
  padding: 0 0 20px;
}
#feature dt {
  background: url(images/top.gif) no-repeat;
  padding: 20px 20px 0;
  font-size: 170%;
  color: #FFF;
  line-height: 1;
  margin: 0;
}
#feature dd {
  padding: 10px 20px 0;
  color: #1B220F;
  line-height: 1.3;
  margin: 0;
}
```

Great! So we've successfully rounded the corners on our definition list. But what if you don't have a definition list? Perhaps you have a **div**, with a headline and paragraph, like this:

sushi-feature.html (excerpt)

```html
<div id="feature">
  <h3>Serving Sushi</h3>
  <p>More traditionally, sushi is served on minimalist
    Japanese-style, geometric, wood or lacquer plates which
    are mono- or duo-tone in color, in keeping with the
    aesthetic qualities of this cuisine. Many small sushi
    restaurants actually use no plates — the sushi is eaten
    directly off of the wooden counter, usually with one's
    hands, despite the historical tradition of eating nigiri
    with chopsticks.</p>
</div>
```

You'll see a distinct similarity between the layout of these elements and those in the previous example: there's a containing block-level element (**div** vs **dl**), an element that contains the headline (**h3** vs **dt**), and an element that holds our content (**p** vs **dd**).

This similarity means that there are literally only two things we have to change in our CSS file in order to make our previous styles work with the new markup. As we referred to the

dl by its **id**, not its element name, we don't even have to make a change to account for this switch. All we need to do is replace the specific references to the **dd** and **dt** elements with references to **p** and **h3**, respectively. Our style sheet should now look like this:

sushi-feature.html

```
* {
  margin: 0;
  padding: 0;
}
html {
  font: small/1.4 "Lucida Grande", Tahoma, sans-serif;
}
body {
  font-size: 92%;
}
#feature {
  background: #96BF55 url(images/bottom.gif) no-repeat bottom
     left;
  width: 220px;
  padding: 0 0 20px;
}
#feature h3 {
  background: url(images/top.gif) no-repeat;
  padding: 20px 20px 0;
  font-size: 170%;
  color: #FFF;
  line-height: 1;
  margin: 0;
}
#feature p {
  padding: 10px 20px 0;
  color: #1B220F;
  line-height: 1.3;
  margin: 0;
}
```

Checking in a browser, which shows us the display in Figure 6.7, we see that our new markup and modified styles work perfectly.

As you can see, the concepts behind the rounded corners style are very portable, and, given the right markup conditions, can be applied very easily.

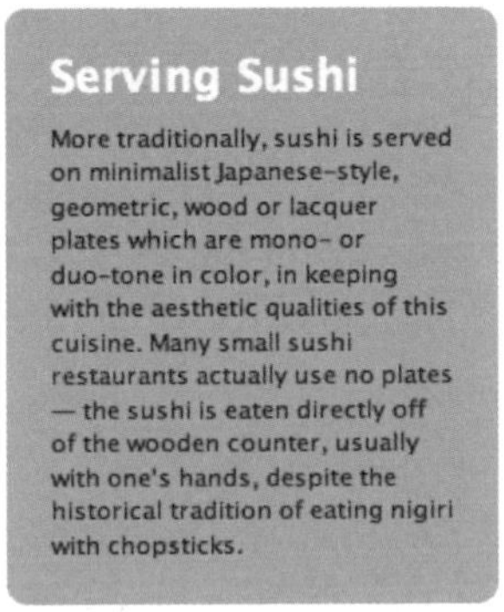

Thinking Forward

You may have noticed this already, but the styles we created in this example already support the inclusion of multiple paragraphs under

Serving Sushi

More traditionally, sushi is served on minimalist Japanese–style, geometric, wood or lacquer plates which are mono– or duo–tone in color, in keeping with the aesthetic qualities of this cuisine. Many small sushi restaurants actually use no plates — the sushi is eaten directly off of the wooden counter, usually with one's hands, despite the historical tradition of eating nigiri with chopsticks.

Figure 6.7: Our new markup and modified styles

the headline. There's always a good chance that you might want to have that capability, so it's best to design your styles accordingly.

Support for multiple paragraphs is accomplished by assigning **`padding`** in the right places. For example, we always want 20px of **`padding`** at the bottom of the box. One method of creating this space would be to put 20px of padding on the bottom of the paragraph element in this example, or the definition description (**`dd`**) in the previous one. However, if we assign the **`padding`** there, adding another paragraph (or definition description, as multiples are allowed) would push the elements 20px apart, not the 10px by which our headline and paragraph are separated. This issue is easily fixed by assigning the 20px of **`padding`** to the bottom of the **`#feature`** selector, instead of to an element contained within. This way, no matter which elements are contained, we can guarantee that the appropriate spacing will be applied.

Now, to ensure the spacing between the paragraphs. Multiple paragraphs need to be separated by 10px of space—the same distance that appears between our headline and paragraph. We've applied even spacing between all our elements, as you can see in Figure 6.8.

Serving Sushi
More traditionally, sushi is served on minimalist Japanese-style, geometric, wood or lacquer plates which are mono- or duo-tone in color, in keeping with the aesthetic qualities of this cuisine.
Many small sushi restaurants actually use no plates — the sushi is eaten directly off of the wooden counter, usually with one's hands, despite the historical tradition of eating nigiri with chopsticks.

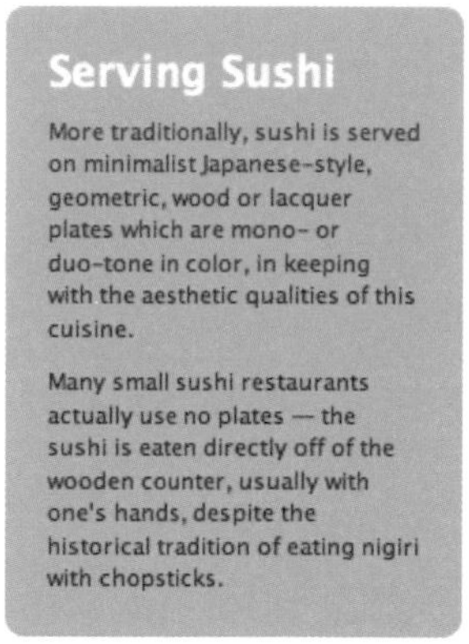

Figure 6.8: Multiple paragraph support for the feature box

Rounding a Layout

Not only are these rounding concepts portable to other feature-type boxes, but they can also be used to round the elements that contain an entire web page layout. Take the mockup shown in Figure 6.9, for example; we meet again our old client from Chapter 4.

CartographyCorner
Home
Maps
Journal
History
References
Contact
BODY CONTENT
SIDEBAR CONTENT
Copyright 2006 - Cartography Corner - All Rights Reserved

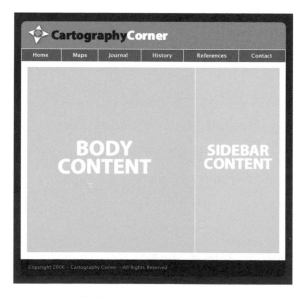

Figure 6.9: Design mockup for our next example

While we're not going to cover the styling of any of the content of this document (if you want to read more about its navigation, see Chapter 4), we will walk through the process of styling the shell. Let's see what the markup for this layout looks like:

fixed-width-layout.html (excerpt)

```
<div  id="wrapper">
  <div id="header">
    <h1>Cartography Corner</h1>
  </div>
  <ul id="navigation">
    …
  </ul>
  <div id="content">
    …
  </div>
  <div id="footer">
    <p>Copyright 2006 - Cartography Corner - All Rights Reserved</p>
  </div>
</div>
```

I've left out of this listing some of the more detailed markup for the areas with which we're not yet concerned. You'll notice that we have a **#wrapper** element that wraps around all our other elements, a header section appropriately identified as **#header**, an unordered list for navigation, and content and footer sections, denoted **#content** and **#footer** respectively. For the purposes of this example, we'll assume that the navigation and content are already styled.

While we'll use the same fixed-width, rounded corner principles we used in the last example, the implementation will be slightly different. Let's start off by assigning the **body** element the main dark **background-color**. We'll give the **#wrapper div** a white **background** and a defined **width**, and align it to the center. In addition, we'll also assign the **#header** and **#footerdiv** elements their background and font colors. I'll be including the same declarations for **margin** properties, **padding**, and fonts as in the previous example:

```
* {
  margin: 0;
  padding: 0;
}
html {
  font: small/1.4 "Lucida Grande", Tahoma, sans-serif;
}
```

```
body {
  font-size: 92%;
  background: #2D2419;
}
#wrapper {
  background: #FFF;
  width: 550px;
  margin: 0 auto;
}
#header {
  background: #A98D71;
}
#footer {
  background: #100D09;
  color: #999;
}
```

We now have a layout that looks like Figure 6.10.

Figure 6.10: Our progress so far

For the header, we'll need an image much like that from the first example, in Figure 6.1. It'll have rounded corners, with a corner color that matches the `background-color` given to the `body` element, and will look like Figure 6.11.

Figure 6.11: The image that will provide the rounded corners for our header

We'll save this image in our *images* folder, name it `header.gif`, and attach it to the header:

```
#header {
  background: #A98D71 url(images/header.gif) no-repeat;
}
```

Our logo file is shown in Figure 6.11; we'll save it in the same place as a GIF image with a transparent background, as `logo.gif`.

We'll replace the `h1` text with this logo image, using the text-indent method covered in Chapter 1.

Figure 6.11: Our logo GIF, with binary transparency

It might look a little ugly here, but when placed over the background color, it'll blend right in—trust me. So let's put the CSS in place:

```
#header {
  background: #A98D71 url(images/header.gif) no-repeat;
}
#header h1 {
  width: 330px;
  height: 56px;
  background: url(images/logo.gif) no-repeat;
  text-indent: -9999px;
  overflow: hidden;
}
```

Now for the footer: we need an image with rounded corners just like the header, but we'll need an inverted version for the bottom of the layout. We'll use the black footer color, which you can see in Figure 6.12, rather than the beige we used for the header. We'll save this as **footer.gif**.

Figure 6.12: The image that will provide the rounded corners of our footer

In the CSS, we add the `background-image`, and apply some appropriate `padding`.

```
#footer {
  background:#100D09 url(images/footer.gif) no-repeat bottom left;
  color:#999;
  padding:10px 15px;
}
```

When we view the page in our browser, we see that our design is complete. The page will expand and contract vertically according to the height of the content, while keeping our rounded corners intact, as shown in Figure 6.13.

Figure 6.13: The finished layout

Great! We can see that, given the constraint of a fixed width, rounding the corners of any element can be simple. All we need are the right hooks on which to hang our background images. Our final CSS file should look like this:

fixed-width-layout.html (excerpt)

```
* {
  margin: 0;
  padding: 0;
}
html {
  font: small/1.4 "Lucida Grande", Tahoma, sans-serif;
}
body {
  font-size: 92%;
  background: #2D2419;
  padding: 20px;
}
#wrapper {
  background: #FFF;
  width: 550px;
  margin: 0 auto;
}
#header {
  background: #A98D71 url(images/header.gif) no-repeat;
}
```

```
#header h1 {
  width: 330px;
  height: 56px;
  background: url(images/logo.gif) no-repeat;
  text-indent: -9999px;
  overflow: hidden;
}
#footer {
  background: #100D09 url(images/footer.gif) no-repeat bottom
    left;
  color: #999;
  padding: 10px 15px;
}
```

Now that we're able to handle vertical flexibility, what if we need the rounded box to expand both vertically *and* horizontally?

Vertical and Horizontal Flexibility

Now that we've become adept at handling vertical flexibility, we know that two images, and therefore two elements, are required to create all four corners. But what if we need the rounded box to expand both vertically *and* horizontally? If horizontal flexibility is added to the parent element, we'll need four separate elements to attach to our four corner graphics, as shown in Figure 6.14.

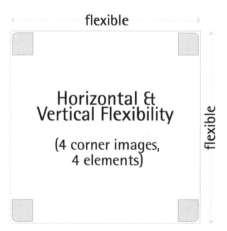

Figure 6.14: Adding rounded corners to container with vertical and horizontal flexibility

One common solution to providing the styling hooks needed for the four images is to add multiple **div** elements around the box to which our background images are attached. But that's not always necessary. Consider our first example of vertical flexibility:

```
<dl id="feature">
  <dt>Roundabout</dt>
  <dd>A roundabout or rotary is a type of road junction (or
      traffic calming device) at which traffic streams around
      a central island, after first yielding (giving way) to
      the circulating traffic.</dd>
</dl>
```

Here we have three block-level elements to work with. We only need one more. Let's add one **div** around the **dl** element, and transfer the **id** attribute to the new **div**:

flexible-roundabout-feature.html (excerpt)

```
<div id="feature">
  <dl>
    <dt>Roundabout</dt>
    <dd>A roundabout or rotary is a type of road junction (or
        traffic calming device) at which traffic streams around
        a central island, after first yielding (giving way) to
        the circulating traffic.</dd>
  </dl>
</div>
```

Let's make this look just like the first example, but add the capability for horizontal expansion based on the browser's font size. We'll translate our previous two background images into four separate corners, and save them as **bottom_left.gif**, **bottom_right.gif**, etc., as depicted in Figure 6.15.

top_left.gif
top_right.gif
bottom_right.gif
bottom_left.gif

Figure 6.15: Four necessary corner images

Now we need to think about where to place our background images. We start by determining which elements will touch which corners, so as to cover them all appropriately. We can determine by looking at the markup that the only element that won't touch the bottom two corners is the **dt** element. The feature **div**, the **dt**, and the **dd** will all extend to the bottom. But similarly, the **dd** will not touch the top two corners, so it must be used on one of the bottom corners. This leaves the **div** and the **dl** to be used in any location.

For this example, we'll use the **div** for the bottom-left corner, the **dd** for the bottom right, the `dl` for the top left, and the `dt` for the top right. As discussed before, we apply the background color to the lowest layer. That means our `div` will have both the background color *and* the bottom-left corner. Enough of the thinking, let's put some of this thought into code:

```
* {
  margin: 0;
  padding: 0;
}
html {
  font: small/1.4 "Lucida Grande", Tahoma, sans-serif;
}
body {
  font-size: 92%;
  background: #FFF;
}
#feature {
  background: #96BF55 url(images/bottom_left.gif) no-repeat
     bottom left;
  width: 20em;
}
#feature dl {
  background: url(images/top_left.gif) no-repeat;
}
#feature dt {
  background: url(images/top_right.gif) no-repeat top right;
}
#feature dd {
  background: url(images/bottom_right.gif) no-repeat bottom
     right;
}
```

As you can see, I've again included the basic page-styling elements at the beginning of the CSS. If we check our code in a browser, we should see something like Figure 6.16.

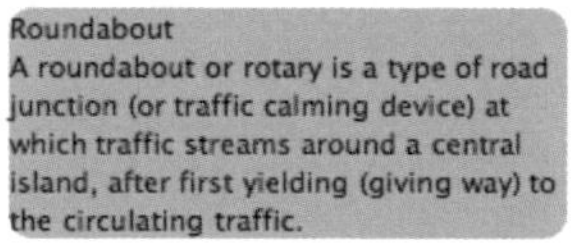

Roundabout
A roundabout or rotary is a type of road junction (or traffic calming device) at which traffic streams around a central island, after first yielding (giving way) to the circulating traffic.

Figure 6.16: Start of our flexible feature box

That's a great result. Because we defined the `width` in `em`s, our `width` is defined by the size of the browser font. Let's see if our element really stretches with the font size like we planned. I'll bump up the font size twice ... and I give you Figure 6.17.

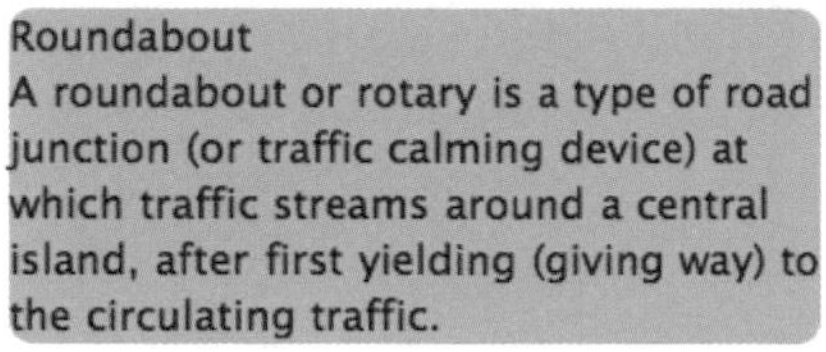

> Roundabout
> A roundabout or rotary is a type of road
> junction (or traffic calming device) at
> which traffic streams around a central
> island, after first yielding (giving way) to
> the circulating traffic.

Figure 6.17: The feature box after the browser's font size is increased

Excellent! Now all that's left is to put in the text styles and `padding`. This exercise will be slightly different from the vertical flexibility example, as we need to be more cautious about how our `padding` is applied—after all, we don't want to push an element away from the corner it's supposed to cover:

flexible-roundabout-feature.html (excerpt)

```
* {
  margin: 0;
  padding: 0;
}
html {
  font: small/1.4 "Lucida Grande", Tahoma, sans-serif;
}
body {
  font-size: 92%;
  background: #FFF;
}
#feature {
  background: #96BF55 url(images/bottom_left.gif) no-repeat bottom left;
  width: 20em;
}
#feature dl {
  background: url(images/top_left.gif) no-repeat;
}
#feature dt {
  background: url(images/top_right.gif) no-repeat top right;
  padding: 1.17em 1.17em 0;
  font-size: 170%;
  color: #FFF;
  line-height: 1;
}
#feature dd {
  background: url(images/bottom_right.gif) no-repeat bottom right;
  padding: 1em 2em 2em;
  color: #1B220F;
  line-height: 1.3;
}
```

We've assigned padding in `ems`, so our box looks consistent as it grows. You might notice the difference in `padding` size between the `dd` and the `dt` elements—this is due to the

ems being units of **font-size**. The **font size** of the **dd** hasn't changed, so it receives **2em** of **padding**. As we increase the **font-size** on the **dt** by **170%**, we need to cut down on the **padding** by the same proportion (100/170), or 59% of our **2em**. This leaves us with a value of around **1.17em**.

Let's see a nice before-and-after comparison of our final product in Figure 6.18 and Figure 6.19.

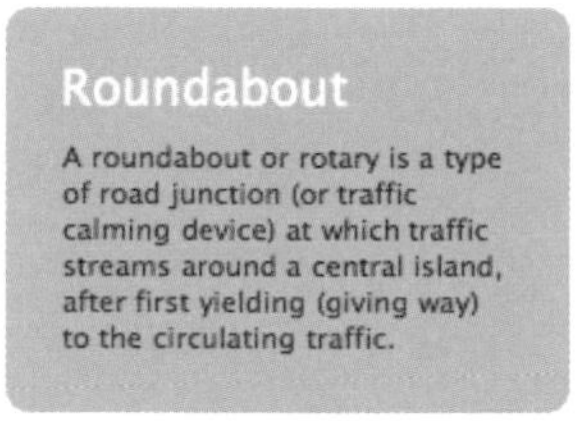

Figure 6.18: Final product at default browser font size

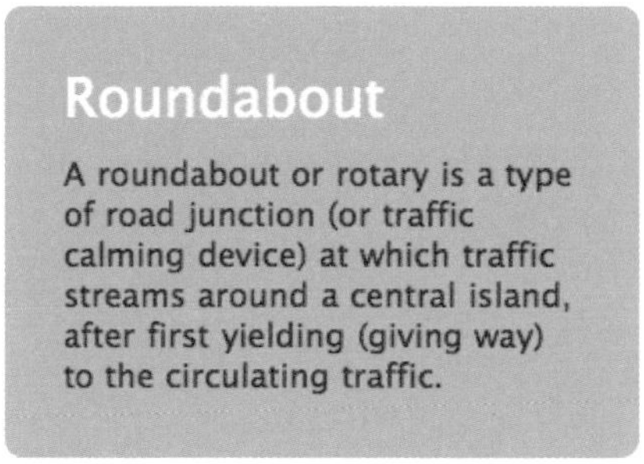

Figure 6.19: ... and with the font size increased

Perfect! Although this more flexible way of styling our rounded box definitely provides some challenges, the basic thought process remains the same. We did, however, have to add one more element to our markup—one that arguably has no semantic value. This addition is the trade-off we have to make with the current limitations (or implementation, if you're the glass-half-full type) of CSS in modern browsers.

This constraint can be seen even more clearly if we examine our second example, which comprised the **div**, headline, and paragraph:

```
<div id="feature">
  <h3>Serving Sushi</h3>
  <p>More traditionally, sushi is served on minimalist
     Japanese-style, geometric, wood or lacquer plates which
     are mono- or duo-tone in color, in keeping with the
     aesthetic qualities of this cuisine. Many small sushi
     restaurants actually use no plates – the sushi is eaten
     directly off of the wooden counter, usually with one's
     hands, despite the historical tradition of eating nigiri
     with chopsticks.</p>
</div>
```

Once again, we have three elements, and we need to add one more to establish the fourth "hook" for the last corner. But in the previous example, it was easier to justify adding the additional **div** element because the outer element was a **dl**. Now, our outer element is already a **div**. We need to take a more careful look at the markup. Are there any other elements that we could add while keeping our markup semantic? For example, could the headline be linked to another page? If so, the added anchor tag would give us the extra hook we need.

But if we can't add anything, we'll have to resort to adding an extra **div** to our existing markup. We really need to evaluate whether our rounded, flexible box is more important than the non-semantic markup we've added. I'm not going to answer that question in any for-once-and-for-all way, because the answer is different for each scenario. The main point to take from this quandary is that it's good practice to always look inside the markup first to see if there are any elements you can take advantage of *before* you begin to add markup.

For this example, I'm going to add the anchor to the headline. Here's what our markup should look like:

flexible-sushi-feature.html (excerpt)

```
<div id="feature">
  <h3><a href="http://en.wikipedia.org/wiki/Sushi">Serving
    Sushi</a></h3>
  <p>More traditionally, sushi is served on minimalist
    Japanese-style, geometric, wood or lacquer plates which
    are mono- or duo-tone in color, in keeping with the
    aesthetic qualities of this cuisine. Many small sushi
    restaurants actually use no plates — the sushi is eaten
    directly off of the wooden counter, usually with one's
    hands, despite the historical tradition of eating nigiri
    with chopsticks.</p>
</div>
```

As we investigate the elements we need to use for each corner, we note that this markup exhibits two main differences from the previous example. Firstly, both the headline and the anchor only touch the top corners, so we need to use the **div** and the paragraph for the bottom corners. Secondly, anchor elements are, by default, inline elements rather than block-level elements, so we'll need to change the value of the **display** property on the anchor to **block**.

To clarify, a block-level element is one that takes up 100% of the available width, much like a **div** or a **p**—it's styled, by default, to have a clear line-break before and after the element, and to fill the horizontal space available. Inline elements might include **a**, **span**, and **strong**. All of these variations wrap with text flow, and inherit their **height** properties from their parent elements' **line-height**s. Block-level elements respond much more predictably to **margin** and **padding** declarations, which is why we need to change our anchor into a block-level element using CSS. Let's see how the CSS departs from that in the previous example:

flexible-sushi-feature.html (excerpt)

```
* {
  margin: 0;
  padding: 0;
}

html {
  font: small/1.4 "Lucida Grande", Tahoma, sans-serif;
}

body {
  font-size: 92%;
  background: #FFF;
}

#feature {
  background: #96BF55 url(images/bottom_left.gif) no-repeat
      bottom left;
  width: 20em;
}

#feature h3 {
  background: url(images/top_left.gif) no-repeat;
}

#feature a {
  background: url(images/top_right.gif) no-repeat top right;
  padding: 1.17em 1.17em 0;
  font-size: 170%;
  color: #FFF;
  line-height: 1;
  display: block;
  text-decoration: none;
}

#feature p {
  background: url(images/bottom_right.gif) no-repeat bottom
      right;
  padding: 1em 2em 2em;
  color: #1B220F;
  line-height: 1.3;
}
```

You can see that, again, not many changes need to be made as the markup is quite similar between the two examples, despite the different names given to the elements. The only addition we needed to make was to apply `display` and `text-decoration` properties to the anchor element, and to swap the `dt` and `dd` for `h3` and `p`. Let's check our browser to see how our changes turned out; Figure 6.20 shows how the feature box should look.

If we increase the font size, as depicted in Figure 6.21, we see that our box grows, yet our corners remain intact.

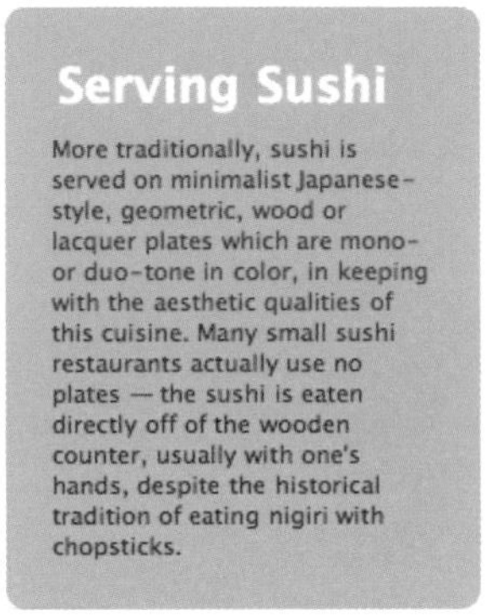

Figure 6.20: Our new flexible version of heading and paragraph

Figure 6.21: Flexible feature box, with increased browser font size

Our rounded corners now work with a fully flexible box! But there are drawbacks to adding horizontal flexibility to our feature element. You'll recall from the first example we saw in this chapter that we coded the CSS in such a way that we could add to the `div` paragraphs that would work properly with paragraph spaces and background images. But, in Figure 6.22, you can see what happens if we create multiple paragraphs using the CSS from this example:

```
<div id="feature">
  <h3><a href="http://en.wikipedia.org/wiki/Sushi">Serving
    Sushi</a></h3>
  <p>More traditionally, sushi is served on minimalist
    Japanese-style, geometric, wood or lacquer plates which
    are mono- or duo-tone in color, in keeping with the
    aesthetic qualities of this cuisine.</p>
  <p>Many small sushi restaurants actually use no plates — the
    sushi is eaten directly off of the wooden counter, usually
    with one's hands, despite the historical tradition of
    eating nigiri with chopsticks.</p>
</div>
```

We've gained an extra corner!

If adding paragraphs is really necessary, we'll have to give the last paragraph some kind of **class** attribute, and add the background image to that element specifically. Alternatively, all the paragraphs could be wrapped in another **div**. But either way, you're complicating your markup and CSS.

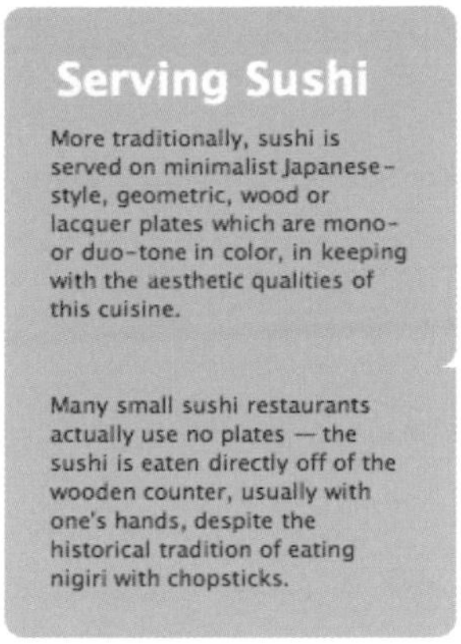

Serving Sushi

More traditionally, sushi is served on minimalist Japanese-style, geometric, wood or lacquer plates which are mono- or duo-tone in color, in keeping with the aesthetic qualities of this cuisine.

Many small sushi restaurants actually use no plates — the sushi is eaten directly off of the wooden counter, usually with one's hands, despite the historical tradition of eating nigiri with chopsticks.

Figure 6.22: Multiple paragraphs cause problems

NOTE   CSS 3 to the Rescue—the :last-child Pseudo-class

When the day arrives that the majority of browsers implement CSS 3 selectors—primarily the **:last-child** pseudo-class[3]—we won't need to choose between the previously mentioned trade-offs. We'll be able to add the bottom-right corner image to the last paragraph using the following CSS:

```
#feature p {
  padding: 1em 2em;
  color: #1B220F;
  line-height: 1.3;
}


#feature > p:last-child {
  padding-bottom: 2em;
  background: url(images/bottom_right.gif) no-repeat bottom
    right;
}
```

No superfluous **div** elements or **class** attributes there!

Again, I'm not going to tell you that any of these options is right or wrong—it's up to you to decide which you'll use. But the rule stands: the more flexible your box, both visually and in terms of its content, the more markup and style you'll have to use to get the desired effect.

---

3   http://www.w3.org/TR/css3-selectors/#last-child-pseudo

Rounding a Fluid Layout

With the previous examples under our belts, let's tackle the task of creating a fluid layout (or, liquid layout): one that expands horizontally based on browser window width. Let's revisit the markup:

flexible-width-layout.html (excerpt)

```
<div  id="wrapper">
  <div id="header">
    <h1>Cartography Corner</h1>
  </div>
  <ul id="navigation">
    …
  </ul>
  <div id="content">
    …
  </div>
  <div id="footer">
    <p>Copyright 2006 - Cartography Corner - All Rights
        Reserved</p>
  </div>
</div>
```

If we evaluate element locations to see which elements we can use for placing the corners, we see that both the header **div** and the **h1** will touch only the top corners. The footer **div** and the paragraph it contains will touch only the bottom corners. The wrapper **div** could be used as a styling hook for any corner, but it doesn't look like we'll need to use it for that purpose. Instead, we'll use it for the expanding white background color.

In preparing the images, we'll need to produce ones that are almost identical to those we used in the previous example, with one major difference. When we styled the **h1** element the last time we used this markup, we included the logo as a background image. Because we can't assign two background images to the same element, let's combine the logo and the top-left corner into one graphic. We'll wind up with a layout that looks like Figure 6.23.

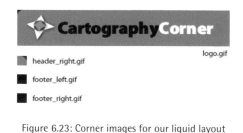

Figure 6.23: Corner images for our liquid layout

To apply these changes in CSS, let's see what needs to be changed from the previous example:

flexible-width-layout.html (excerpt)

```css
* {
  margin: 0;
  padding: 0;
}
html {
  font: small/1.4 "Lucida Grande", Tahoma, sans-serif;
}
body {
  font-size: 92%;
  background: #2D2419;
  padding: 20px;
}
#wrapper {
  background: #FFF;
  min-width: 550px;
  width: 80%;
  margin: 0 auto;
}
#header {
  background: #A98D71 url(images/header_right.gif)
      no-repeat top right;
}
#header h1 {
  width: 330px;
  height: 56px;
  background: url(images/logo.gif) no-repeat;
  text-indent: -9999px;
  overflow: hidden;
}
#footer {
  background: #100D09 url(images/footer_right.gif) no-repeat
      bottom right;
  color: #999;
  /* Padding was removed from the footer element… */
}
#footer p {
  padding: 10px 15px; /* … and placed here inside the
      paragraph */
  background: url(images/footer_left.gif) no-repeat bottom
      left;
}
```

We can see, once again, that the changes required to make the rounded layout flexible in both directions are really very simple. If you have enough markup to work with, as we do in this case, the process of attaching background images becomes trivial. The hardest aspect of making your rounded corners fully flexible is having the markup handy. Once that's in place, it's smooth sailing. How do our changes look in a browser? Let's check out Figure 6.24.

Figure 6.24: Our fluid layout at its minimum width

If we stretch the browser window, we'll see in Figure 6.25 that our layout grows right along with it.

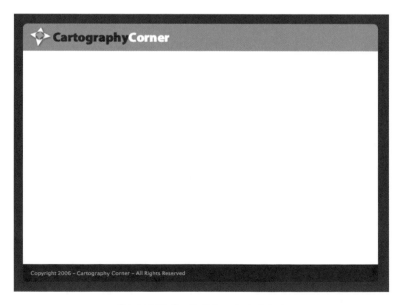

Figure 6.25: Our fluid layout, stretched

Experimenting with these Techniques

While this chapter has focused on adding rounded corners to content boxes, the techniques we've discussed could be used to achieve various decorative effects, like the one demonstrated in Figure 6.26.

Figure 6.26: Using rounded corner techniques to add a decorative border

The markup, styles, and images I've used in this layout are included in the code archive in case you'd like to take a closer look. As with all elements of design, the possibilities are up to you!

Summary

The central theme reiterated throughout this chapter is that rounding corners can be a very simple process. But if certain permises are not met, it can easily become a non-semantic tag soup. This unhappy scenario can be avoided if you follow a few simple steps that I've outlined in this chapter.

We've found that we need to determine whether the flexibility required in a layout or design is vertical, horizontal, or a combination of both. Our markup must be evaluated to determine whether we need to compromise its semantic purity, or simply retain what we already have. When we come to creating the images, careful planning is required to reduce the need to insert additional elements. And in applying the styles, we need to be aware of usability and flexibility, and of potential problems, such as that exemplified with our use of padding.

Finally, keep in mind that with great power comes great responsibility. Rounded corners should be used sparingly, and for a certain effect. When utilized with discretion, rounded corners lend themselves to the successful production of softer, more usable interfaces. But when overused, well ... consider the fate of the once-popular but now much-abused drop shadow. You get the picture!

7

Tables

Have you waded knee-deep into web standards and thought you'd never again encounter a `table` element? Tables may have been rejected as "bad" and "evil," due to their past misuse as a layout element, but the web standards movement hasn't quite eliminated them from the planet. In fact, all the proliferation of semantic markup has done is send tables back to doing what they do best: presenting tabular data.

While tabular data (and the spreadsheet horrors of which it probably reminds you) may not always seem to be the most exciting material, working with tables gives us plenty of opportunity to break out some serious CSS skills and create some fantastic looks—even while adding a dash of usability.

Header	Header	
You can span	You can sp.	
	It's like a pu	
	This way.	T
		W
		I?

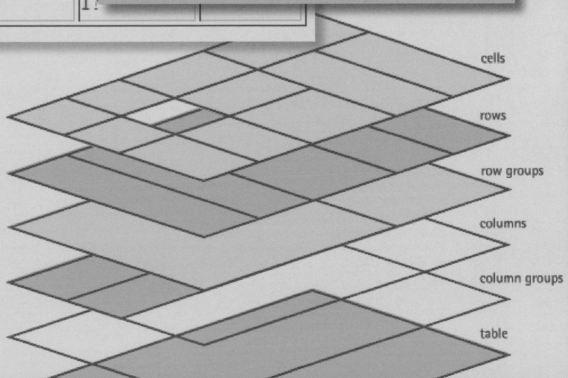

cells

rows

row groups

columns

column groups

table

In this chapter, we'll spend some time gaining an understanding of the elements that go into the construction of a table. After we set this foundation, we'll look at the various styles that can be applied to those table elements. Along the way, we'll deal with the cross-browser problems that are sure to crop up at this moment in web history. With the theory out of the way, we'll reach some practical examples of how our tables can be made both functional and attractive, and become acquainted with some of the niceties a dash of JavaScript can offer to the humble table. Finally, we'll look to the future to predict how CSS 3 will affect our table-designing efforts.

The Structure

Styling tables can be liberating and confusing at the same time. While the many potential elements of a table offer plenty of ways to tie in some additional style, cross-browser inconsistencies and the lack of support for some truly useful CSS selectors can prove to be frustrating roadblocks.

However, before we tackle the intricacies of styling a table, let's go over all the different potential elements of a table. Much of this will probably be familiar ground, but there might be a couple of new elements that you haven't encountered before. My apologies if this groundwork comes across as a little dry, but it's well worth your attention. Think of table-styling as a roller-coaster; you've gotta spend time on the long, slow ascent before you get into the wild ride of styling!

I'm sure all the tables you've put together up until now utilized at least three basic elements: `table`, `tr`, and `td`—table, row, and data cell respectively. Likewise, you've probably used or seen the `th`, the header cell. Your markup may have looked something like this:

table-example-basic.html (excerpt)

```
<table>
  <tr>
    <th scope="col">Person</th>
    <th scope="col">Web Site</th>
  </tr>
  <tr>
    <td>Bryan Veloso</td>
    <td><a href="http://avalonstar.com/">Avalonstar</a></td>
  </tr>
  <tr>
    <td>Dan Rubin</td>
    <td><a href="http://superfluousbanter.org/">
      SuperfluousBanter</a></td>
  </tr>
</table>
```

Those aren't all the elemental components of a table, though. We also have the **thead**, **tbody**, **tfoot**, **caption**, **col**, and **colgroup** elements at our disposal. These elements serve a very semantic purpose, each of which I'll explain in a little detail so you'll know which to use and when. Each of these elements will provide a point where we can hook in some CSS styling to take our table from being a boring blackspot on our page to being a mini work of art in its own right.

The `table` Element

A table isn't a table without a **table** element. It all starts from here.

A **table** has a number of attributes, such as **border**, **cellpadding**, and **cellspacing**, all of which you've used often if you've emerged from the tables-for-layout school of web design. We can ignore **border** and **cellpadding** for now, as we can replicate these attributes in CSS. One presentational attribute we'll need to keep handy is **cellspacing**. Internet Explorer doesn't support the ability to handle **cellspacing** via CSS, which means that if we need to maintain control, we'll have to do it at the HTML level.

In addition to those attributes, we also have the **frame** attribute and the **rules** attribute. The **frame** attribute controls the display of the outermost border on the table. Its possible values are **void**, **above**, **below**, **hsides**, **vsides**, **lhs**, **rhs**, **box**, and **border**. The default value is void: this will remove the border from around the table.

The border manifests itself differently in each of the four browsers I used to test this markup:

- Internet Explorer rendered a three-dimensional border on all sides.
- Firefox rendered a gray border on the left and top, with black on the right and bottom.
- Opera rendered a solid black border.
- Safari rendered no border at all.

When Internet Explorer is given a value other than **void**, this browser will incorrectly render a border on the cells inside the table as well. For example, if you specify **lhs**, the left side of each cell will be rendered:

```
<table frame="lhs">
```

Firefox and Opera render this markup correctly, as shown in Figure 7.1.

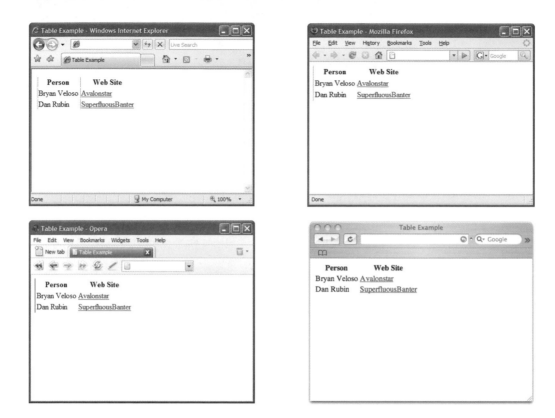

Figure 7.1: Table with **frame="lhs"**, as rendered by Internet Explorer, Firefox, Opera, and Safari

The **rules** attribute, which controls how the dividing borders of the table should be drawn, has five valid values: **none**, **groups**, **rows**, **cols**, and **all**. If a value of **none**—the default value—is specified, no lines will be drawn between the cells.

An interesting point to note here is that if you fail to specify a **rules** attribute, the **border-style** (using CSS) you've set for **colgroup** elements or **col** elements will be ignored. But if you specify a value of **none**, suddenly the **border-style** comes to life.

A value of **groups** will apply a border (gray and beveled in Internet Explorer, 1px and black in Firefox and Opera) around each **thead**, **tfoot**, **tbody**, and **colgroup**. Setting **rules** to **rows** or **cols** will apply a border between each respective row or column, while **all** will apply a border around every cell. Again, if the **frame** attribute is omitted and **rules** is set to any value but **none**, IE breaks from the pack and displays a border around the entire table. As was the case with the **frame** attribute, Safari doesn't support the **rules** attribute. Output rendered by the current versions of the four most common browsers can be seen in Figure 7.2.

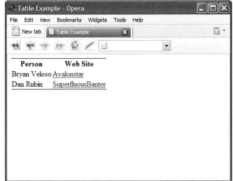

Figure 7.2: Comparing **frame="hsides"** and **rules="groups"** applied to **table**

If you wish to use the **frame** or the **rules** attribute, it's best to use them together, as frustrating rendering bugs can result if they're used independently.

The **caption** Element

A **caption** is intended to display a summary of what the table is about and, by default, it appears centered above the table as seen in Figure 7.3. A **caption** doesn't have any special attributes, which makes our styling fairly straightforward.

The **caption** element appears right after the **table** tag:

```
<table frame="hsides" rules="groups">
  <caption>Sites that I like to visit</caption>
```

Sites that I like to visit

Person	Web Site
Bryan Veloso	Avalonstar
Dan Rubin	SuperfluousBanter

Figure 7.3: Default display of the **caption** element in Firefox

The `thead`, `tbody`, and `tfoot` Elements

The `thead`, `tbody`, and `tfoot` elements are called **row groups**. Their function is to group rows together. A `table` can have only one `thead` and one `tfoot`, but it can have multiple `tbody` elements. Here's an example to demonstrate the intended use of these elements:

table-example.html (excerpt)

```
<table frame="hsides" rules="groups">
  <caption>Sites that I like to visit</caption>
  <thead>
    <tr>
      <th scope="col">Person</th>
      <th scope="col">URL</th>
    </tr>
  </thead>
  <tfoot>
    <tr>
      <td colspan="2">[1] Enjoys Dance Dance Revolution</td>
    </tr>
  </tfoot>
  <tbody>
    <tr>
      <td>Bryan Veloso [1]</td>
      <td><a href="http://avalonstar.com/">Avalonstar</a></td>
    </tr>
    <tr>
      <td>Dan Rubin</td>
      <td><a href="http://superfluousbanter.org/">
        SuperfluousBanter</a></td>
    </tr>
  </tbody>
</table>
```

As you might notice from this example, the footer actually appears before the body. Take a look at Figure 7.4 to see how it looks in the browser, though, and you'll notice that the footer is positioned at the end of the table, where it belongs. "What gives?" you ask, quite reasonably. The specification was designed this way to allow a `table` to be rendered before the entire body of content was received.

Sites that I like to visit	
Person	**Web Site**
Bryan Veloso [1]	Avalonstar
Dan Rubin	SuperfluousBanter
[1] Enjoys Dance Dance Revolution	

Figure 7.4: `tfoot` displayed at end of table, despite source order

All row groups support the **align** and **valign** attributes. The **align** attribute adjusts the horizontal alignment whereas **valign** handles the vertical alignment. Don't worry too much about these attributes, as we'll handle them in CSS using the **text-align** and **vertical-align** properties.

The **tr** Element

A **tr** is a table row. Rows are much like row groups, in that they both support **align** and **valign** attributes. Table rows also have the **bgcolor** attribute that allows a background color to be set. Again, we'll handle this step in CSS.

The **th** and **td** Elements

The **th** and **td** elements are the table cells, and hold the data for the **table**. Table cells have a congregation of attributes, many of which are important not only from a style perspective, but also from an accessibility standpoint.

Like the row and row groups, table cells have **align** and **valign** attributes, as well as **rowspan** and **colspan** attributes. The **rowspan** attribute indicates how many rows high the cell should be, including the current cell. The **colspan** is very similar, concerned with—you guessed it—the width of the columns. Check out Figure 7.5 to see how columns and rows can be spanned.

Figure 7.5: **colspan** and **rowspan** attributes at work

Now here's the markup that produces Figure 7.5:

```
                                            colspan-rowspan.html (excerpt)
<table>
  <thead>
    <tr>
      <th scope="col">Header</th>
      <th scope="col">Header</th>
      <th scope="col">Header</th>
      <th scope="col">Header</th>
    </tr>
  </thead>
```

```
<tbody>
  <tr>
    <td rowspan="6">You can span down.</td>
  </tr>
  <tr>
    <td colspan="3">You can span across.</td>
  </tr>
  <tr>
    <td colspan="2">It's like a puzzle.</td>
    <td rowspan="4">Over here.</td>
  </tr>
  <tr>
    <td rowspan="3">This way.</td>
  </tr>
  <tr>
    <td>That way.</td>
  </tr>
  <tr>
    <td>Where am I?</td>
  </tr>
</tbody>
</table>
```

The **th** element may also contain the **axis**, **headers**, **scope**, and **abbr** attributes, each of which allows you to create relationships between the various cells. Screenreaders can use some of these attributes to improve a reader's ability to navigate the **table**. It's difficult to target specific elements via the presence of these attributes, due to browser support for some CSS selectors, but I mention them here for the sake of completeness. If you'd like to learn more about these attributes, check out the W3C specification.[1]

The `col` and `colgroup` Elements

I've saved the best for last! **col** is used to identify a column; **colgroup** identifies groups of columns. As far as styling is concerned, the greatest benefit of these two elements is that they allow us to style entire columns without resorting to the addition of a **class** to every cell in the column.

Spanning can be assigned to our **colgroup** elements and **col** elements. This assignation doesn't actually collapse multiple cells into one, as would the **rowspan** or **colspan** attributes on a cell. It simply provides a shorthand way of specifying attributes to be applied across multiple columns:

---

1   http://www.w3.org/TR/html4/struct/tables.html#h-11.2.6

```
<colgroup>
  <col />
  <col />
</colgroup>
<colgroup>
  <col />
  <col />
  <col />
</colgroup>
```

This can also be written as follows:

```
<colgroup span="2" />
<colgroup>
  <col span="2" />
  <col />
</colgroup>
```

The `span` attribute on the `colgroup` indicates that the `colgroup` spans two columns. The `col` elements aren't used when a `span` attribute is present on a `colgroup`. If `col` elements do exist in a `colgroup`, the `span` attribute on the `colgroup` is ignored. The `span` attribute on the `col` element also indicates that there are two columns.

The `width` attribute can be specified using one of the three formats:

■ `width="100"`
width in pixels

■ `width="20%"`
width in percentage

■ `width="2*"`
relative width indicating that the cell should be twice as wide as a regular cell[2]

Using a percentage or relative `width` in Internet Explorer expands the overall table to 100%, whereas Firefox, Safari, and Opera collapse to the smallest area required to fill the cells—the expected behavior.

Here's an example that demonstrates a number of the structural attributes we've just covered, including how it is displayed in Firefox (the end result of which you can see in Figure 7.6):

2   This relative sizing doesn't work in Internet Explorer or Opera, so it's best avoided.

```
<table>
  <caption>Growth Chart</caption>
  <col width="60%">
  <col width="20%">
  <col width="20%">
  <thead>
    <tr>
      <th scope="col">Name</th>
      <th scope="col">Age</th>
      <th scope="col">Height</th>
    </tr>
  </thead>
  <tfoot>
    <tr>
      <td colspan="3">[1] Has <a
          href="http://en.wikipedia.org/wiki/Gigantism">
          Gigantism</a></td>
    </tr>
  </tfoot>
  <tbody>
    <tr>
      <th rowspan="3" align="left">Albert</th>
      <td>1</td>
      <td align="center">2 ft. 8 in.</td>
    </tr>
    <tr>
      <td>10</td>
      <td align="center">4 ft. 6 in.</td>
    </tr>
    <tr>
      <td>20</td>
      <td align="center">6 ft. 1 in.</td>
    </tr>
  </tbody>
  <tbody>
    <tr>
      <th rowspan="3" align="left">Betty [1]</th>
      <td>1</td>
      <td align="center">2 ft. 3 in.</td>
    </tr>
    <tr>
      <td>10</td>
      <td align="center">4 ft. 2 in.</td>
    </tr>
    <tr>
      <td>20</td>
      <td align="center">7 ft. 2 in.</td>
    </tr>
  </tbody>
</table>
```

Growth Chart		
Name	**Age**	**Height**
Albert	1	2 ft. 8 in.
	10	4 ft. 6 in.
	20	6 ft. 1 in.
Betty [1]	1	2 ft. 3 in.
	10	4 ft. 2 in.
	20	7 ft. 2 in.
[1] Has Gigantism		

Figure 7.6: Preceding markup as rendered by Firefox

You've endured the slow, steep ascent and learned how to create a table; it's almost time for that roller-coaster ride I promised at the start of the chapter! We'll plunge into that styling right after we have a look at the CSS properties we need.

The Styling

Before we dive into some practical examples, it's important to understand which CSS properties we can actually make use of and where we can use them. We'll look at styles specific to the **table** element, columns, and captions. After that, we'll learn how backgrounds are handled. From there on in, it's all fun—we'll go through some examples to demonstrate what can be done to bring a little art to the science of tables.

Using the **table** Element

Several properties are unique to the **table** element:

- **border-collapse**
- **border-spacing**
- **empty-cells**

The **border-collapse** property can have a value of either **separate** or **collapse**, as demonstrated in Figure 7.7. The default property is **separate**, but it creates tables that look fairly chunky. Using **collapse** removes the space between the cells, effectively overriding any cell spacing that may be set in the HTML. This step will make our tables look cleaner, so it's a good move to start with.

Figure 7.7: Comparing **separate** and **collapse** values of **border-collapse** property

> **NOTE Issues with Collapsing Borders**
>
> Collapsing the border will create issues if you have borders between two cells where each cell has different border styles. A border conflict resolution guide that explains how these conflicts should be resolved is available from the W3C.[3]

When setting the **`border-spacing`** property of a **`table`**, you can specify either one or two length values. If only one is specified, the value affects the spacing on all sides. If two values are specified, the first specifies the horizontal spacing (left and right of the cell) and the second specifies the vertical spacing (above and below the cell):[3]

```
table {
  border-spacing: 2px 5px;
}
```

This example adds 2px of vertical space and 5px of horizontal space between each cell.

The color that appears in the space is always that of the table background. Setting the row or cell background will never change the color between the cells.

Our nemesis Internet Explorer, however, doesn't support the **`border-spacing`** property, even in IE7. The only course of action this situation leaves us with is to use the **`cell-spacing`** attribute in HTML to achieve the same effect as **`border-spacing`**.

The **`empty-cells`** property has two values: **`show`** and **`hide`**, the rendering of which can be seen in Figure 7.8.

This property determines whether a border will be visible on an empty cell; it can be applied to almost any element within a **`table`**, such as specific rows or cells. Once again, however, Internet Explorer doesn't support the **`empty-cells`** property.

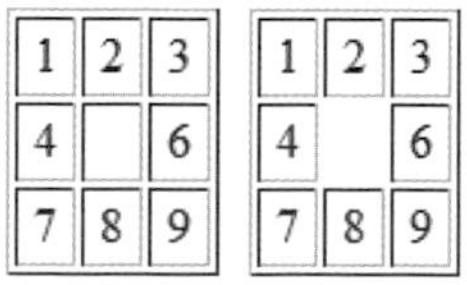

Figure 7.8: Values for **`empty-cells`** property—**`show`** on left and **`hide`** on right

Setting Column Styles

The column group elements (**`colgroup`**) are unique in that cells don't actually inherit anything from them. Therefore, there are only four properties that *are* applicable to

3 http://www.w3.org/TR/CSS21/tables.html#border-conflict-resolution/

colgroup: **border**, **background**, **width**, and **visibility**. The use of these properties results in inconsistencies across the browsers, as demonstrated in Figure 7.9, so be prepared!

The **border** property works well in Firefox and Safari. In Opera, applying **border** to a **col** element with a **span** attribute set on it doesn't apply the **border** to each column as it does in Firefox or Safari. In Internet Explorer, the **border** CSS property doesn't work at all.

Here's how we go about setting table borders and **border-collapse** in CSS:

```css
table {
  width: 400px;
  border-collapse: collapse;
}
#test {
  border: 1px solid blue;
}
```

... and modifying our HTML to disable the **border** attribute:

```html
<table border="0">
  <caption>Growth Chart</caption>
  <col width="60%">
  <col width="20%" id="test">
  <col width="20%">

...
```

The **border-collapse** needs to be set to **collapse** for the border to show in Firefox and Safari.

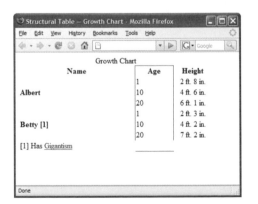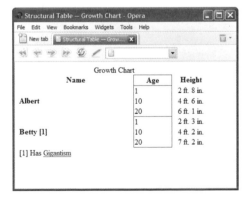

Figure 7.9: Comparison of column border rendering in Firefox and Opera

The **background** property is fairly consistent across browsers, but it still has its little quirks. A **background-image**, for example, applied to a column group is set as the background to each column in Opera, but is incorrectly applied to each separate cell in Safari and Internet Explorer. There are also layering issues that only Firefox can cope with sufficiently. With any luck, you'll never run into these layering issues, but I'll cover these in a little more detail in the section called "Applying Successful Backgrounds" below.

The `width` property works well in all browsers tested. Keep in mind that when applied to a `colgroup`, the `width` affects the size of each column contained within that `colgroup`. For example, if you set a `width` of 200px on a column group that contains two columns, then each column is 200px, reaching a total of 400px for the column group.

Finally, `visibility` is included just for completeness, but Firefox is the only browser that currently supports it. `visibility` can be set to `collapse`, which prevents the column from being seen.

Formatting Captions

The `caption` elements can be formatted like most other block elements, including properties like `text-align` and `font-weight`. There's an additional CSS property that can come in very handy, and that's `caption-side`. This property can be set to either `top` or `bottom`, which will allow the caption to appear either above or below the table respectively. Firefox takes it a step further and supports values of `left` or `right`. I hate to sound like a broken record, but good ol' Internet Explorer doesn't support `caption-side`.

Applying Successful Backgrounds

Since we're talking about backgrounds on columns, let's delve a little deeper into how backgrounds on tables should work. Essentially, different elements act as layers. Any transparency on one level reveals the background of the level below it. Figure 7.10 shows a W3C diagram that demonstrates the layering of backgrounds on table elements.[4]

However, as you may have noticed with some of the cross-browser issues I mentioned before, most browsers don't handle backgrounds like the specification suggests. Many actually take any backgrounds specified at the column or row level and simply apply them at the cell level. When using patterned backgrounds, this can prove *extremely* frustrating—any repeating patterns fail to line up. Playing with the opacity at the cell level also reveals how badly Safari, Opera, and Internet Explorer get it wrong. As an example, have a look at Figure 7.11, which demonstrates a background being applied to a table row. Albert displays correctly in Firefox, but he's in real trouble when displayed in Internet Explorer.

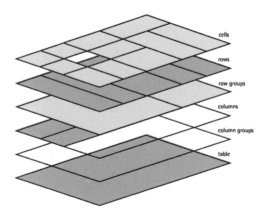

Figure 7.10: The W3C's schema of table layers

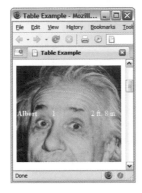 

Figure 7.11: **td background** comparison between Firefox and Internet Explorer

Unfortunately, table usage just isn't as popular as it used to be, so we'll most likely be waiting a very long time for this problem to be rectified in the rest of the browsers.

Luckily, the application of a **background** on the **table** element does work consistently. The background should tile properly across the entire table and behave exactly as it should. Let's give this application a shot, and see whether Albert can avoid being fragmented when he encounters the rigors of being displayed in Internet Explorer.

If our table and columns were of a fixed **width**, we could actually get around the cell **background** issues by offsetting the **background** for each column. It's a tedious task, but it's well worth it, so let's dive in! Here's an example to demonstrate this approach:

background-position.html (excerpt)

```
table {
  width: 223px;
}
td {
  background: red url(images/albert.jpg) repeat 0 0;
  height: 200px;
}
td.col1 {
  width: 90px;
}
td.col2 {
  background-position: -90px 0;
  width: 43px;
}
td.col3 {
  background-position: -133px 0;
  width: 90px;
}
```

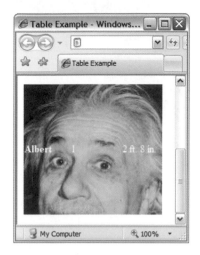

Figure 7.12: Resolved Internet Explorer example

Each column after the first is simply shifted over by the width of the previous cells. The first column doesn't need to be shifted, whereas the second requires shifting over the width of the first column. Finally, the third column background has to be shifted over the total width of the first two columns. Figure 7.12 shows Albert in Internet Explorer again, but with the **background** shifted within each cell—he's much happier.

Well, that's all, folks. For the minute, anyway. This understanding of column, caption, and background styles set us up well for that roller-coaster ride—now it's time for us to look at some practical applications of all the styling we've learned!

Table Elements in Action

With all the details out of the way, let's take a look at some examples of tables—how spiffy can we make them with the careful application of the styling we've learned?

Adding Style to Tabular Calendars

Calendars love tables. In fact, the two are a match made in heaven, what with calendars adapting their weeks so well to a series of rows, and their days to columns. Figure 7.13 shows a completely unadorned **table**.

	June					
Sun	Mon	Tue	Wed	Thu	Fri	Sat
1	2	3	4	5	6 It's my birthday!	7
8	9	10	11	12	13	14
15	16	17	18	19	20	21
22	23	24	25	26	27	28
29	30					

Figure 7.13: Unstyled calendar

This is an okay and perfectly functional table, except that it's arguably a bit dull; my need to promote my birthday has thrown out the balance just a smidgen, too. Let's take a look at the markup and think about what it'll take to give this table a bit more style and je ne sais quoi:

calendar.html (excerpt)

```
<table>
  <caption>June</caption>
  <col class="weekend" />
  <col class="weekday" span="5" />
  <col class="weekend" />
  <thead>
    <tr>
      <th>Sun</th>
      <th>Mon</th>
      <th>Tue</th>
      <th>Wed</th>
      <th>Thu</th>
      <th>Fri</th>
      <th>Sat</th>
    </tr>
  </thead>
  <tbody>
    <tr>
      <td><div class="day">1</div></td>
      <td><div class="day">2</div></td>
      <td><div class="day">3</div></td>
      <td><div class="day">4</div></td>
      <td><div class="day">5</div></td>
      <td class="birthday"><div class="day">6</div>
          <div class="notes">It's my birthday!</div></td>
      <td><div class="day">7</div></td>
    </tr>
    [ … ]
  </tbody>
</table>
```

We'll specifically add a `div` around each day number. This allows additional items to be added to a day, and leaves us the flexibility of styling the number itself. More general styles, such as holidays, are applied to the table cell—let's apply an appropriately stand-out style to my birthday!

To make this look more like a calendar, we can set up a number of styles. We'll style a larger `caption`, causing the month to stand out more prominently. Each day is given a `height` and `width`, allowing room to add notes. The weekend columns have been set up to stand out from weekdays, and we can designate holidays and birthdays as special.

Here's the CSS for our calendar table:

calendar.html (excerpt)

```css
table {
  border: 1px solid #999;
  border-collapse: collapse;
  font-family: Georgia, Times, serif;
}
th {
  border: 1px solid #999;
  font-size: 70%;
  text-transform: uppercase;
}
td {
  border: 1px solid #999;
  height: 5em;
  width:5em;
  padding: 5px;
  vertical-align: top;
}
caption {
  font-size: 300%;
  font-style: italic;
}
.day {
  text-align: right;
}
.notes {
  font-family: Arial, Helvetica, sans-serif;
  font-size: 80%;
  text-align: right;
  padding-left: 20px;
}
.birthday {
  background-color: #ECE;
}
.weekend {
  background-color: #F3F3F3;
}
```

Once we've combined our modified markup and the style sheet, we get Figure 7.14, a much more aesthetically pleasing calendar.

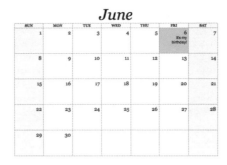

Figure 7.14: Styled calendar

Striping Table Rows

Striping, also known as **zebra tables**, is useful on large, monotonous sets of data as it helps improve readability. Too much text without delineation can make it difficult to see where one column lines up with another within a particular row.

To achieve striping, we simply add a **class** to every other row (check out Figure 7.20 at the end of this chapter for an even cooler, although less supported, approach to striping):

```
…
<tr>
  <td>…</td>
  <td>…</td>
  <td>…</td>
</tr>
<tr class="even">
  <td>…</td>
  <td>…</td>
  <td>…</td>
</tr>
…
```

Our base styles would be applied to the normal **tr** and then alternate styles applied to the **tr** elements that have a **class** of **even**:

striped.html (excerpt)

```
tr {
  background-color: #FEE;
}
tr.even {
  background-color: #EEF;
}
```

In this example, the odd rows will be a light red and the even rows will be a light blue, as shown in Figure 7.15.

Article	Date
24 ways to feed a goat	October 2
Top 10 ways to become popular	October 4
Site taken? Get to the point.	October 8
I was crazy to say yes	October 9
Trying too hard	October 15
Not trying hard enough	October 23
Are you dressing up?	October 30
Happy Halloween!	October 31
8 articles for October	

Figure 7.15: Different **background-color**s on alternate rows for an easier-to-read table

Another option I often choose when striping my tables is to use a semi-transparent PNG as a background image for the alternate rows, as I've done in Figure 7.16. Taking this route allows me to change out the **background-color** (or **background-image**) on the **table** without having to worry about sizing or color-matching issues:

striped-png.html (excerpt)

```
tbody tr.odd td {
  background: transparent url(images/tr_bg.png) repeat
    top left;
}
```

Article	Date
24 ways to feed a goat	October 2
Top 10 ways to become popular	October 4
Site taken? Get to the point.	October 8
I was crazy to say yes	October 9
Trying too hard	October 15
Not trying hard enough	October 23
Are you dressing up?	October 30
Happy Halloween!	October 31
8 articles for October	

Figure 7.16: Striping alternate rows using a semi-transparent PNG

PNG, pronounced "ping," is an image-format type just like GIF or JPG, but it also supports a graduated transparency. In other words, the **background** can be made partially visible through parts of the image, like looking through a foggy glass window. Conversely, GIF only supports index transparency where there are no levels of opaqueness—it's either on or it's off. JPG doesn't support transparency at all. Most graphics software, such as Adobe Fireworks, The GIMP, or Adobe Photoshop, will happily export PNGs, so it's a very useful image format to have up your sleeve.

I normally export a PNG that is just white and is set to a transparency of about 15% to 25%, as this provides a semi-transparent overlay that'll work in the context of almost any color scheme.

As discussed in Chapter 2, Internet Explorer didn't support PNG background images prior to version 7. Once again, we'll work around the problem by using Internet Explorer's proprietary conditional comments:

striped-ong.html (excerpt)

```
<!--[if lt IE 7]>
  <style type="text/css" media="screen">
    tr.even {
      background: none;
      filter: progid:DXImageTransform.Microsoft.AlphaImageLoader
        (src='images/tr_bg.png', sizingMethod='scale');
    }
  </style>
<![endif]-->
```

"But, hang on a second," you ask. "Why use a PNG instead of the opacity CSS property?" Well, setting opacity in CSS might seem like the obvious choice for achieving this effect; the trouble is, it applies the opacity to all elements contained within. Therefore, all text and images would also be see-through. Setting opacity on an element requires some additional trickery to make it compatible with Internet Explorer, as well as causing your CSS to be invalid—unless the proprietary **filter** property is set via IE conditional comments:

```
td {
  opacity: 0.2;
  filter: alpha(opacity=20);
}
```

The **opacity** property is supported in Safari, Firefox, and Opera, and is part of the CSS 3 specification.[5] To accomplish the same result in Internet Explorer, you have to use the proprietary **filter** property, which lets you specify an **alpha filter**.

You've stuck with me this far into the chapter, so it's time I let you in on a little secret of mine. One trick I've often used is to have an image applied to the **table background** that eventually fades off to a solid color:

```
table {
  width: 450px;
  color: #FFF;
  background: #333 url(images/table_bg.png) no-repeat top left;
  border-collapse: collapse;
  border: 8px solid #9C0;
}
```

---

5   http://www.w3.org/TR/css3-color/#opacity/

This small exercise can give your table some crazy flair while still being an extremely solid cross-browser solution. Using this effect, in combination with the alpha PNGs, can allow you to create some very sexy tables!

The `background-image` is set on the `table`, which, as we covered in Chapter 3, is reliable across all browsers. The image is specifically designed to fade out at the bottom to a solid color, which you can see in Figure 7.17, where the example fades to a solid gray.

Article	Date
24 ways to feed a goat	October 2
Top 10 ways to become popular	October 4
Site taken? Get to the point.	October 8
I was crazy to say yes	October 9
Trying too hard	October 15
Not trying hard enough	October 23
Are you dressing up?	October 30
Happy Halloween!	October 31
8 articles for October	

Figure 7.17: Combining alpha-PNG row striping with gradient background

So, there it is—I'm sure you'll agree that a bit of CSS, judiciously applied, can make the most boring calendar bounce into a layout worthy of a wallplanner, with styling that allows latitude for creativity. Likewise, striping is a simple enough application, but produces a great effect that can be widely used in many table applications to give the most pedestrian content a colorful edge. It doesn't end there, though.

Using JavaScript

As you've seen so far, CSS is fantastic for giving our tables some sexy sizzle. What can *really* send our tables over the edge is some nice JavaScript!

If you've been developing with web standards for some time, you've most likely come across this mantra: separate your presentation from your content. There's a third spoke to this web-standards wheel, and that is **behavior**. Behavior is best handled through **unobtrusive JavaScript**. Unobtrusive JavaScript is having your scripts reside in an external file (just like a style sheet) that hooks itself into your HTML document.

Using unobtrusive JavaScript keeps your HTML clean and easily accessible, even for those users who don't have JavaScript or have it turned off. The content itself will still be available and accessible for these users, who are, after all, in the minority; meanwhile, those users who have JavaScript turned on will be able to take advantage of the additional features you've enabled.

So, what can JavaScript do to pretty up our tables?

Row and Column Highlighting

A common feature is to add row highlighting support for Internet Explorer 6 (and earlier). We can also take it to the next level and add column highlighting for all browsers.

If JavaScript isn't your thing and the code in this example doesn't make much sense, that's okay. If you're interested in learning JavaScript, I recommend that you grab a copy of the SitePoint book *The JavaScript Anthology: 101 Essential Tips, Tricks, & Hacks*, which is an essential text in this area.[6]

Let's define a function that will run when the page loads. Thinking about our logic, we want this function to run any time a user moves the mouse over the table. More specifically, when the mouse is over a specific cell, it should change the **background** for that row and that column.

The first thing we need to do is to grab the **table** element and pass it into our highlight function.

scripts/highlight.js (excerpt)

```
window.onload = function()
{
  var tbl = document.getElementById('mytable');
  setHighlight(tbl);
}
```

I've used **window.onload**, which is a really quick way to say that this block of code should run when the **window** has finished loading. Now, let's see what the setHighlight function looks like.

scripts/highlight.js (excerpt)

```
function setHighlight(table)
{
  if (!table) return;
  var TDs = table.getElementsByTagName("td");
  for(var i = 0; i<TDs.length; i++) {
    TDs[i].onmouseover = rowColHighlight;
    TDs[i].onmouseout = rowColDelight;
  }
}
```

Our highlight function will return to its origin if an element isn't passed through to the function. If we have an element, it'll attract all table cells within our **table**. It loops

---

6   James Edwards and Cameron Adams, *The JavaScript Anthology: 101 Essential Tips, Tricks, & Hacks*, SitePoint, 2006. http://www.sitepoint.com/books/jsant1/

through them and attaches two events to each one. The `rowColHighlight` will be responsible for highlighting rows and columns when the user moves a mouse over a cell, and `rowColDelight` will be responsible for removing the highlight when the user moves the mouse out of a cell.

scripts/highlight.js (excerpt)

```
function rowColHighlight()
{
  highlighter(this, '#EEE');
}
function rowColDelight()
{
  highlighter(this, '');
}
```

Our two functions just call another function but pass in two variables. The first is the element to be highlighted. The `this` keyword refers to the element that triggered the event—in our case, it's the cell. The second variable is the color that we want for the highlighter.

The highlighter function is our meat and potatoes:

scripts/highlight.js (excerpt)

```
function highlighter(cell, color)
{
  cell.parentNode.style.backgroundColor = color;
  var table = getTable(cell);
  var col = table.getElementsByTagName("col");
  col[cell.cellIndex].style.backgroundColor = color;
}
```

First, from the cell, we tell it to get the `parentNode` (the row element surrounding my cells) and change the `background-color` to the color that was passed in. Then, we tell it to get the `table` that surrounds the cell. Retrieving the `table` element can be a little trickier depending on how the HTML is set up, so we've created another function to handle this. I'll touch on this again shortly.

Once we have our `table` element, we grab all the `col` elements in the table and then grab the one that matches the column in which the cell resides. The `cellIndex` property is the number of columns up to and including the current cell. Once we have the right column, we assign it a style. This styling should work as long as no `background` is specified on the other cells, rows, or row groups.

Back to the getTable function that I skipped before:

```
                                                    scripts/highlight.js (excerpt)

function getTable(obj)
{
  while (obj && obj.tagName.toLowerCase() != 'table')
  {
    obj = getTable(obj.parentNode);
  }
  return obj;
}
```

This function takes the current element and checks to see whether it's the **table** element. If it isn't, then the function grabs the parent element and checks that. This checking process will continue until the function finds the **table** element or no element at all. Once the **table** is found, that **table** object is returned.

Figure 7.18 depicts our highlighting function in action.

Table 1: Census Information

Name	Age	Gender
Jonathan	32	Male
Michelle	30	Female
Hayden	2	Male

Figure 7.18: Row and column highlighting compatible with most browsers

I should point out that the script makes a number of huge assumptions. To make your code more reliable, you should provide checking mechanisms to account for different scenarios. For example, one of the assumptions we've made here is that there would be the same number of **col** elements as there are cells in a row. This may not be the case if you used **colgroup** elements or the **span** attribute on other **col** elements. If any of those assumptions were incorrect, you'd be bound to see JavaScript errors.

Other Ideas

One of the other common responsibilities often relegated to JavaScript is **table sorting**. Table sorting is a very handy tool for your users, allowing them to manipulate the table view without requiring slow and repetitive page refreshes from the server. A quick search on Google for "table sorting" will yield a number of scripts; I've used Stuart Langridge's "sorttable script" with much success.[7]

---

7   http://kryogenix.org/code/browser/sorttable/

With the onslaught of **Ajax**—the ability to connect to and send and receive data from the server via JavaScript—you can even offer **spreadsheet-like functionality** including live editing. For a great example, check out Active Widgets Grid component.[8] Speaking of things new and cutting-edge, by the way, what about CSS 3? Let's indulge in some speculation about how this upcoming standard will revolutionize the way we style our tables.

The Future

Styling our table was easy enough, but you might have found some of the steps redundant, such as applying a `class` to every second row to create a striped table. Luckily, within the drafts of the new CSS 3 specification lie a number of useful selectors that will simplify our lives considerably.

> **NOTE   *Browser Support Conundrum***
>
> Some browser developers like those behind Firefox and Opera have been pushing ahead and trying to include early support for many of the useful things within the CSS 3 specification. Internet Explorer, however, is behind, surprise, surprise. Unfortunately, this fact means that with IE still being the browser of choice for the majority of web users, widespread adoption of CSS 3 support features is likely to be limited.

Probably the most exciting and most useful selector when it comes to styling tables are the child pseudo-selectors, of which there are several.

The `:nth-child(an+b)` selector allows you to select every nth element. Essentially, **a** divides the set of elements and **b** is the offset. Remember our striped tables? Here's how you'll be able to style every second row with a different color:

```
tbody:nth-child(2n) { … } /* even rows */
tbody:nth-child(2n+1) { … } /* odd rows */
```

Alternatively, you could use the `:nth-of-type(an+b)` selector to accomplish the same thing:

```
tr:nth-of-type(2n) { … }
tr:nth-of-type(2n+1) { … }
```

Likewise, if you needed to style every second column with a different color, you could apply the style on every second **td** element:

```
tr:nth-child(2n) { … }
td:nth-of-type(2n) { … }
```

---

8   http://www.activewidgets.com/grid/

By providing a value of **0** for **a**, the offset allows you to select the **n**th element. For example, if you wanted to style just the fifth column:

```
tr:nth-child(0n+5) { … }
td:nth-of-type(0n+5) { … }
```

Both **nth-child** and **nth-of-type** are very similar but will give you fantastic control when it comes to styling your tables.

There's also a glimmer of light at the end of the IE tunnel. Internet Explorer 7, recently released, has support for a number of new selectors, including **:first-child** and sibling selectors that allow us to mimic **nth-child**. The sibling selector uses the plus sign (**+**) to target elements. Therefore, if you wanted to style the second column from the left, as shown in Figure 7.19, you'd use the following:

```
td:first-child + td {
  background-color:#036;
}
```

Sites that I like to visit

Person	URL
Bryan Veloso [1]	http://avalonstar.com/
Dan Rubin	http://superfluousbanter.org/
[1] Enjoys Dance Dance Revolution	

Figure 7.19: Using **td:first-child+td** to alter **background-color**

The **td:first-child** will target the first cell within a row and then the sibling selector (the **+** sign) targets the element right beside it. If you wanted to target the fourth column you'd use the following:

```
td:first-child + td + td + td {
  background-color:#036;
}
```

Imagine a table, with a number of values, where you want the last column to be bolded to indicate that the data is a sum. Using the **:last-child** selector will do the trick:

```
td:last-child { … }
```

Taking advantage of **:first-child** and **:last-child**, you could expand on the striped **table** that we saw earlier to add rounded corners to the first and last cells of both the header and the footer. The border is an image set as the **background-image** of the first and last cells within each row.

Figure 7.20: Using CSS 3 selectors to add rounded corners to **table**

There are plenty more selectors that you can expect to see in the not-too-distant future. Although we're probably a few years away from being able to use some of these features in all popular browsers, it never hurts to dream. For more information on the CSS 3 selectors, check out the relevant section of the W3C CSS 3 specification.[9]

Summary

I hope you've finished this chapter with a newfound respect for tables. With any luck, I've shown you a few **table** elements you weren't aware of before.

We've discovered how to create a perfectly semantic data table that provides lots of hooks for our CSS. We've set up a well-structured **table** and learned to style it effectively. We've learned that giving a table some style actually makes our table more useful, making it easier to read and understand the data contained within.

We've seen how JavaScript can inject a little personality and some additional usability without making things difficult for those users who don't have JavaScript. Hopefully, you've gained some valuable ideas on how to implement JavaScript on tables in new and useful ways.

We've envisaged the future, and it's bright! We've anticipated how the new features of CSS 3 will offer us easy ways to make our tables look good, and now we have the knowledge to use them as they become available.

Congratulations, your CSS training is complete! Whatever challenges you may face— problems with headings, images, backgrounds, navigation, forms, content containers, or even tables—you have the skills to overcome them. With this expertise, and a little creative flair, you can make your mark creating attractive, usable designs.

---

9   http://www.w3.org/TR/css3-selectors

Index